baby beanies

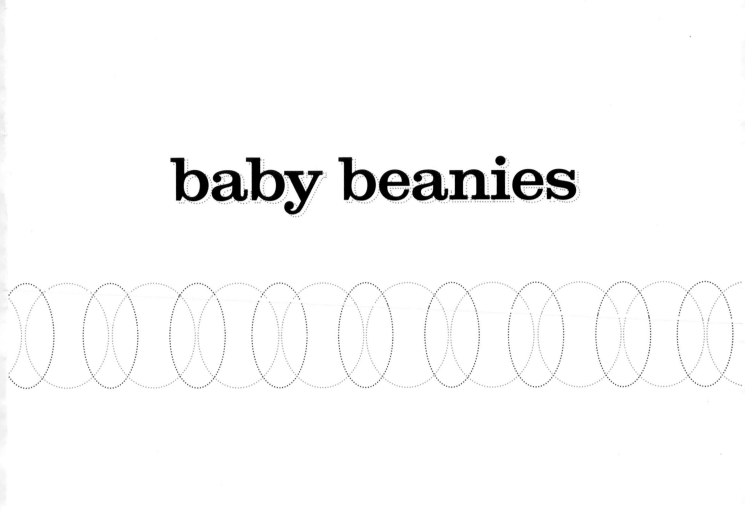

baby beanies

HAPPY HATS TO KNIT FOR LITTLE HEADS

Amanda Keeys

Watson-Guptill Publications / New York

Senior Acquisitions Editor: Julie Mazur
Editor: Linda Hetzer
Designer: 3&Co.
Production Manager: Salvatore Destro

First published in 2008 by Watson-Guptill Publications,
Crown Publishing Group
a division of Random House Inc.,
New York, NY
www.crownpublishing.com
www.watsonguptill.com

Library of Congress Cataloging-in-Publication Number: 2007942906

ISBN-13: 978-0-8230-9903-0
ISBN-10: 0-8230-9903-2

Printed in China

First printing, 2008

3 4 5 6 7 8 / 15 14 13 12 11 10 09

To my own four goobers: Jakob, Madison, Isaiah, and Lilly. Thank you for being my inspiration, always. And to Matt, for the endless cups of coffee and putting up with more insane yarn ramblings than any one should ever have to endure in a single lifetime. xoxo.

contents

introduction

i started knitting for one reason: to make beautiful baby hats. As a professional children's photographer, I have an obsession with having a range of cute and quirky caps for children to wear in the photographs I take. There is nothing cuter than a little one wearing a knit on their noggin! But the problem was, I wasn't having much success finding hats that would look good in photos. I wanted something with great texture, fun color, and, really, I didn't want the hats to look perfect and store-bought. They needed to have some attitude, a bit of whimsy, and be able to complement the character of the child wearing it. So picking up the needles myself was my next best option.

I had actually been taught to knit before. Several times, at least. By my nan and my mum as a little girl, and then in my teenage years, by my future mother-in-law. It didn't stick, though. Inevitably I'd become frustrated at my lack of skill and the clumsy stitches I was producing or grow bored with the miles and miles of plain garter stitch scarf that was supposed to be the perfect beginner's project.

With the help of various books and websites, I finally taught myself how to knit while pregnant with my youngest daughter. I wanted to make cute little hats for her newborn photographs, but I never managed to find a pattern I liked or that was easy enough for me to finish with my very limited knitting skills. Fast-forward a few months, and I finally decided to just grab my needles and a ball of yarn and knit a hat. No pattern. No real clue what I was doing. But somehow, it worked. And from the moment that tiny little hat was formed, I was HOOKED. I could not stop making hats!

It was soon apparent that not only did my children have more hats than they could ever possibly wear (not even counting the ones I'd bought before I started making them), but that I had more than enough for any photo shoot I might have. So, what to do? Fellow photographers urged me to start selling them online, which I did, and I was amazed by the response. It turns out I wasn't the only one looking for fun, colorful, whimsical baby hats! And before I knew it, I was opening up an email asking me if I was interested in writing a book!

One of the best parts of knitting is the online knitting community. It is huge. So many websites, blogs, podcasts, and forums devoted to knitting are out there. And so many fellow knitters, happy to share advice, feedback, encouragement, and camaraderie. It's easy to feel overwhelmed and lonely

9

baby beanies

spending nearly every day at home with my kids, but the knitting community helps me feel like I am part of something. I can go onto a forum and chat about what I am working on, show off my new yarn purchase, or just chat with others about our days (and kids!). In short, it has opened up a whole new world to me—and it can for you, as well.

Hats are perfect for beginning knitters, as well as for anyone who has a little one in his or her life and enjoys quick, fun knitting projects. They're small, usually quick to knit, and an easy way to try out new skills without investing loads of time and money. They're wonderful presents, whether for your own child, a grandchild, or as a quick shower gift for a friend.

My hats are playful and whimsical, sometimes adorable and sometimes serious, just like the babies I photograph wearing them. I've tried to make them slightly unusual and off-center, to give them just that little something to make them—and the little heads they cover—stand out.

I hope you will enjoy knitting these hats as much as I have enjoyed creating them. Be prepared to be inundated with admiring comments when your little one wears the hat out in public!

FINDING TIME TO KNIT

In this age of multi-tasking, Blackberries, and play-dates, who has time to knit? As a mother of four, this is a challenge I face constantly. As soon as I pick up the needles—or even head in that direction—a chorus of, "Mum, Mum, Mum, Mu-u-um, MUM!" starts up and I'm dragged away to whatever urgent matter my children have concocted. And just when I think I've finally got a moment, it's time to make snacks, grab a drink, or put someone in the bath. There's always homework to help with, books to read, toys to play with, babies to snuggle, and children to tuck into bed. And before I know it, an entire day has passed in a whirl of activity. And yet, I still find time to knit. I make the time.

I keep my knitting in a bag that I can easily cart around the house. If I'm watching the kids play outside, I take the bag with me. Maybe I'll only get a chance to finish a row, but that's still one row. If I'm giving the kids a bath (and not working with a yarn that will be ruined by a little splash of water), I plop down on a stool with my knitting close at hand. When my youngest daughter, Lilly, was a baby, she practically lived in her sling (a pouch-style carrier I used for several months). She slept so well in this sling that I was often able to knit uninterrupted for hours before she stirred. I can't knit this way anymore, even though Lilly still enjoys being carried in the sling. She has what I call grabby hands: She'll yank and pull and fight tooth-and-nail to possess whatever it is I'm holding/working on/doing.

Whether your life is busy with little ones or other equally pressing demands, find your own way to insert knitting into the nooks and crannies of your life. Bring it with you on the bus or train, while you wait at the dentist, or while you talk on the phone with a friend. Take ten minutes before starting the next thing on your to-do list, or before going to bed at night. Think of your knitting time as a little break, a chance to spend some time doing something creative just for you. Relax and unwind, and make something beautiful at the same time.

gearing up

All you really need to knit—if you're determined to use whatever's on hand—are two sticks and some string. But most of us prefer a pair of knitting needles and some yarn. And while everything else is optional, it's handy to have an assortment of basic tools and materials on hand to make things easier.

needles

Before I learned to knit (and I mean *really* learned to knit, not just the horrid wonky scarves of my childhood) I thought all knitting needles were pretty much the same. Now I know better! You can buy needles in straight and circular or with a point at both ends (called double-pointed needles, or DPNs). There are plastic, metal, and wooden needles in different lengths and sizes. I prefer silver-plated brass needles, as they are light and smooth and very quiet, which is handy when knitting near a sleeping baby! Choose whatever material feels best, and don't be afraid to experiment with different kinds of needles for different yarns.

To make a baby hat, you either knit on straight needles and bother with all that fussy seaming or you knit "in the round" on circular needles. I hadn't even heard of circular needles until, with a simple hat pattern in hand, I went to ask my mother-in-law for advice. She showed me lots of circular needles with tiny points and super-long cables, and I wondered how on earth you could knit something small enough to fit a baby on something so huge. Then I discovered yarn stores (a whole store devoted to yarn—heaven!) and learned all about circular needles. As it turns out, you want to use something smaller for a baby hat. So, in this book you will use a 16-inch (40 cm) circular needle. This is the length of the needle. The other number you need to remember is the actual needle size, or width of the needle. For these hats, I use either a size 7 (4.5 mm) or size 9 (5.5 mm) needle. When there are too few stitches to continue knitting comfortably on a circular needle, you will have to switch to double-pointed needles (DPNs) of the same size as the circular needle.

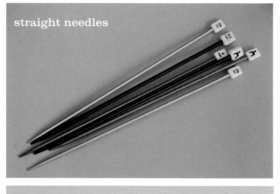

straight needles

double pointed needles (or DPNs)

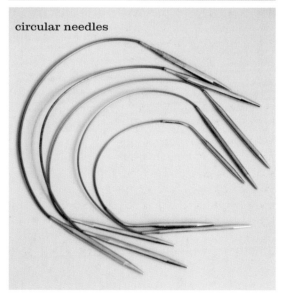

circular needles

yarn

This wonderful stuff comes in all sorts of delicious colors, textures, weights, and fiber combinations to suit your every mood.

color

Color is very personal. Although I have suggested certain colors for each pattern, you can work with your own preferences and pick out colors to suit your chosen recipient. Maybe baby won't glow in orange and pink and you'd prefer soft gray and blue? Go with it! The colors are suggestions only and are meant as a jumping-off point for your own creativity.

fiber

Yarn is available in natural fibers, such as cotton, wool, silk, and mohair; synthetic fibers, such as acrylic, nylon, and polyester; and combinations of both. I far prefer natural fiber yarns—they breathe and have a liveliness to them in a way that man-made fibers don't. Plus, I just think they feel better. Wool is fantastically warm in winter and comes in about any color you can imagine because it holds dye so well. I remember horrible, itchy sweaters from my childhood, but most wool yarns today are lovely and soft. Merino wool is especially light and soft and a perfect choice for babies. While cotton isn't as forgiving as wool in terms of elasticity and springiness, it's nice and cool in summer and great for those living in warmer climates (like me!). You can usually put a cotton garment straight into the washing machine, too, which is an added bonus.

TIP: If you use acrylic yarns, keep in mind that acrylic will melt when exposed to fire, so never leave a baby unattended or put them down to sleep wearing something knitted from acrylic yarn.

15

weight

Yarn comes in a variety of weights, or thicknesses. Fingering, baby, sport, DK (for "double knitting"), worsted, Aran, chunky, bulky . . . the list goes on. Different weights are better suited for different projects—you wouldn't, for example, want to knit a warm winter hat in thin fingering yarn.

The Craft Yarn Council of America has developed a standardized system for yarn weights, shown below, with symbols used throughout the industry. For this book I have used only DK and worsted weight yarns.

texture

Smooth, silky, soft, fluffy, light, rough—the list is endless! Yarns with fluffy tufts, nubby tweeds, or smooth and shiny ribbon strands are best saved for when you have a few projects under your belt and feel confident working with yarn and needles. I made the mistake of making my first scarf in a fluffy, thick ropelike novelty yarn, and it was a disaster. The fluff made the stitches hard to see and the thick ropey yarn was hard for a beginner to work with. For your first projects, go with a simple, smooth yarn to make it easier to see and feel your stitches as you work.

YARN WEIGHT CATEGORY	Super-Fine	Fine	Light	Medium	Bulky	Super-Bulky
SYMBOL	1 SUPER FINE	2 FINE	3 LIGHT	4 MEDIUM	5 BULKY	5 BULKY
TYPES OF YARN	Sock, fingering, baby	Sport, baby	DK, light worsted	Worsted, afghan, Aran	Chunky, craft, rug	Bulky, roving
NUMBER OF STITCHES IN 4 INCHES OF KNITTED FABRIC	27–32 sts	23–26 sts	21–24 sts	16–20 sts	12–15 sts	6–11 sts
RECOMMENDED NEEDLE SIZES (US)	1–3	3–5	5–7	7–9	9–11	11 and larger
RECOMMENDED NEEDLE SIZES (METRIC)	2.25–3.25mm	3.25–3.75mm	3.75–4.5mm	4.5–5.5mm	5.5–8mm	8mm and larger

READING A YARN LABEL

Most yarn comes wrapped in a label that will tell you lots of helpful things about the yarn.

Quantity:

The label will tell you how much the ball or skein weighs (in ounces and/or grams) and how much yarn it contains (in yards and/or meters). This information is important when it comes to figuring out how much yarn you need for a project, especially if you're substituting the yarn called for in the pattern.

Fiber content:

The label tells you what kind(s) of fiber the yarn is made from and, if it's a blend, in what proportion.

Dye lot:

Yarn is dyed in limited quantities at one time, and there can be minor variations between dye lots. So, if you need more than one skein, make sure you buy skeins of the same color yarn from one dye lot.

Gauge and needle size:

The gauge is the number of stitches and rows in a 4-inch square, using the recommended size needles. (More about this on page 23.) Since each person knits differently—more loosely or tightly—the needle size called for on a yarn label is only a suggestion.

Care instructions:

The label explains how to wash the items made from the yarn, usually shown in symbols. It's a good idea to follow these instructions; you want to take good care of the hat you just created!

yarn substitutions

At the beginning of every pattern I have listed the yarn I used. Because the only two yarn weights used are DK and worsted, it's easy to substitute another yarn of the same weight. Also, if you have leftover yarn from one hat, you can easily use it in the next one.

In the back of the book, on page 143, you can find out where online to buy the yarns I've used. If you want to use something else, take a look at the yarn specifics. If the yarn is the right weight, texture, and has the same yardage per ounce, you'll be fine.

I find that cotton droops a lot more than wool, so when knitting with cotton, I tend to knit a size smaller. If substituting wool yarn for cotton, you might want to knit a size larger. I am not very fussy about gauge when it comes to hats. I figure that if it's too small, I can save the hat as a gift for a newborn baby, and if it's a little too big, well, they can always grow into it.

yarn winder

stitch markers

yarn storage

helpful extras

Here are some more odds and ends I have found helpful in my knitting adventures.

yarn winder

This is an amazing little contraption that you use to wind your yarn into a manageable ball. If you can, buy one of these fabulous little things early on. I cannot tell you how frustrating it is to wind yarn by hand with the skein hooked over your knees, trying not to turn the whole thing into a tangled mess.

stitch markers

These are typically little circles of plastic that you use to mark your place. Some have an open end so you can attach them to a stitch, some are closed circles that slip on and off the ends of your needles, and some have a little locking catch so you can use them either way. You can buy beaded markers or make your own out of jewelry wire and beads. And, in a pinch, you can always use a loop of scrap yarn as a marker.

knitting bag

You must have a knitting bag! You want one large enough to hold the project you're working on, extra yarn, and whatever tools you need. I have tried many different types of bags, totes, and satchels. The one I like best is a very large fabric handbag with lots of little pockets that I picked up at a market for a few dollars. It comfortably holds a couple of projects, whatever needles I need (and a few spare), a notebook and pen, and all the other bits and pieces I keep on hand.

place to store yarn

I keep my yarn in boxes and bags, lining shelves, placed in bowls, and filling a whole cupboard dedicated to my yarn collection (aka, my stash). If you have little children, it is a good idea to store your yarn where it can't be reached, such as in a box with a locked lid, in a cupboard, or in a basket on a high shelf. I can tell you from first-hand experience that walking in to find your sweet one-year-old in a tangled heap of yarn, grinning up at you and obviously pleased with her efforts, while cute in an "Oh my goodness, I can't believe she did that" kind of way, will send you into a freakout.

CARING FOR YOUR HATS

An easy tip for caring for your hand-knit hats is to keep a note of the care instructions that came on the yarn label.

Fiber content:

Most hats made of acrylic or acrylic blend and cotton yarns can be put straight into the washing machine (though maybe not the dryer). Hats made of wool and other natural fibers require a little more care.

Handwash:

Handwash your knits in cool water with soap flakes or a small amount of liquid soap made especially for wool. Gently submerge the knitting in the water and allow it to soak if necessary. Now gently squeeze out the excess water (be careful not to twist or wring the fabric). I like to rinse with clear, cold water to remove any traces of soap that might remain. Squeeze out the excess water again. Place the hat between two thick towels and squeeze to remove as much water as possible. Lay the hat out flat until completely dry.

Gift label:

If you are giving the hat as a gift, write these instructions on a pretty piece of notepaper or a card and slip it in with the gift so the recipient won't inadvertently shrink the hat by using hot water.

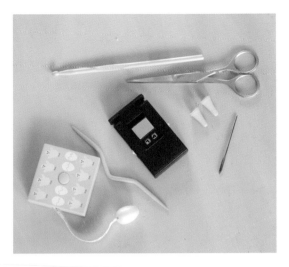

Clockwise from top: crochet hook, scissors, point protectors, tapestry needle, row counter, cable needle, and tape measure.

other tools

Since these items are small, pop them in a small bag so you can transfer them to whatever knitting bag or project you're working on.

- tape measure
- notebook and pen
- sharp darning needles or tapestry needles (to weave in yarn ends and for seaming)
- small, sharp scissors
- calculator
- row counter
- crochet hook (to pick up dropped stitches)
- cable needle
- little, rubber point protectors

getting started

What is knitting? To create knitted fabric you will manipulate loops of yarn to form rows of interlocking stitches. You need only a very basic knowledge of knitting stitches—simply knit and purl—and you have the tools literally in your hands to create just about anything. Since teaching myself to knit, friends often comment, "Wow, you knit? Isn't that hard?" The answer is, in short, no.

reading patterns

Each pattern in this book starts by listing the same things: the skills you need to know to make the hat; the needles, yarn, and other tools you'll need; the gauge (shown opposite); sizing information; and then the pattern itself. Be sure to skim through the pattern before starting to make sure you're familiar with the basic terms and stitches. If not, you may want to return to this chapter and practice unfamiliar stitches on scrap yarn first.

Each pattern has sizes for 0–6 months, 6–12 months, 1–2 years, and 2 years and up. The smallest size is given first; successively larger sizes follow in parentheses. Specific directions for each size are given in the same sequence throughout the pattern. It can be helpful to go through the pattern first and highlight the directions for your size, so you don't accidentally knit the wrong number of stitches.

Knitting patterns use a standard set of abbreviations. Once you become familiar with them, you'll be able to read any knitting pattern. Here are the basic abbreviations used in this book.

TIP: If a pattern uses more than one color of yarn, the colors are indicated with letters A, B, C, and so on. The colors of the yarn are listed in the materials list followed by the letter, usually in parentheses. The letter is then used throughout the pattern.

ABBREVIATIONS

**	repeat steps between asterisks as many times as noted
BO	bind off
C	cable
CN	cable needle
CO	cast on
DPN	double-pointed needle
k	knit
k2tog	knit 2 stitches together (decrease)
k3tog	knit 3 stitches together (decrease)
kfb	knit into front and back of same stitch (increase)
LH	left-hand
m1	make 1 stitch (increase)
mb	make bobble
p	purl
p2tog	purl 2 together (decrease)
psso	pass slipped stitch over
RH	right-hand
sl1	slip 1 stitch
sl1kw	slip 1 knitwise
sl1pw	slip 1 purlwise
wyib	with yarn in back
wyif	with yarn in front
yo	yarn over

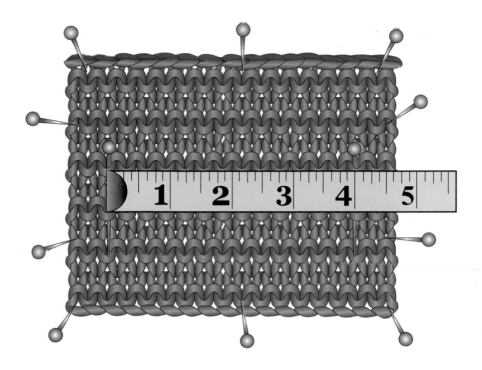

gauge

Your knitting gauge is how many stitches and rows per inch of knitted fabric you produce with a given needle size. You measure this quite simply by knitting a square swatch and then counting how many stitches and rows you have in 1 inch. This is important because if your gauge is looser than called for, your hat will be too big. If it is tighter than called for, you may well end up with a hat that will barely fit a doll.

How to measure your gauge:

1. Knit a sample swatch, a piece approximately 5 inches square, using the yarn from your project and the needle size called for in the pattern.

2. Without stretching the swatch, pin it down to an ironing board so that it lays nice and flat.

3. With a ruler, count the number of stitches in a 1-inch section. You may like to measure this a couple of times in different places just to be sure.

4. Refer back to the pattern gauge. If your gauge is tighter (more stitches per inch than called for), use a larger needle size and swatch again. If your gauge is looser (fewer stitches per inch than called for), use a smaller needle size and swatch again. Continue to swatch until you achieve the gauge called for in the pattern.

the basic stitches

All knitting patterns are made up of knit and purl stitches. When knitting on straight needles, you work across all of the stitches on one row and then turn the needles around to begin your next row. With circular needles, you knit in rounds. Instead of turning your work when you reach the end of the round, you simply keep going, building upon each previous round in a continuous circle. Note that all directions are given for a right-handed knitter. If you're left-handed, just switch them.

casting on

The first step is to get the yarn on the needles, and it's called "casting on." There are many ways to do this; I use the long-tail cast-on throughout this book. Once you get the technique down, casting on should feel like you're making a smooth figure-eight motion.

1. Start by measuring the length of yarn needed for the number of stitches you need to cast on (the pattern will tell you how many). To do this, wrap the yarn once around the needle for every stitch, then add several extra inches. Once you have done this once or twice, you will be able to gauge more or less accurately the length of yarn needed for casting on. I have found that most of the time I can cast on by measuring two arms' lengths of yarn.

2. Make a slipknot at the "working end" of your length of yarn (the end closest to the ball of yarn). Slide the slipknot onto your needle, pulling the yarn "tail" to tighten. The slipknot will count as your first stitch.

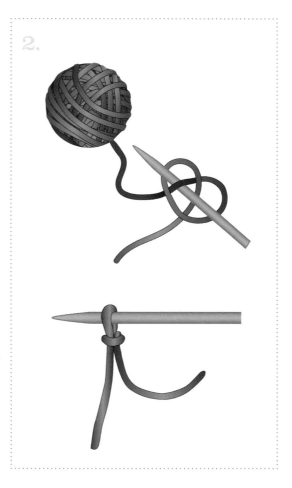

2.

3. Hold the tail of the yarn draped over your thumb and the yarn coming from the ball draped over your index finger. Use your lower fingers to hold the yarn tight against your palm. Now turn your hand so your palm is facing almost toward you.

4. Holding the needle in your right hand, scoop the tip of the needle under the yarn tail over your thumb, then scoop it up and under the yarn coming over your index finger.

5. Bring the loop of yarn from your thumb over and onto the needle. Remove your thumb and tug gently on the yarn tail to tighten the stitch.

6. Repeat steps 4–5 to cast on the required number of stitches.

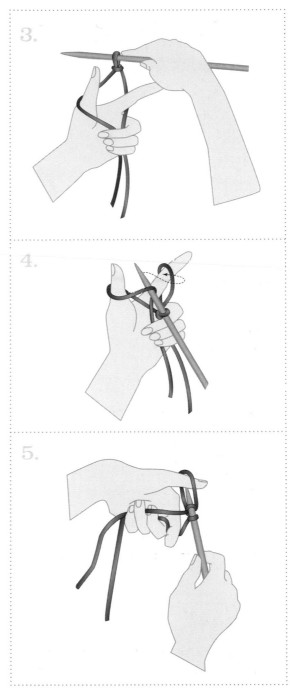

the knit stitch (k)

The knit stitch is the main, and the most basic, of all knitting stitches. It is probably the easiest stitch to learn.

1. Hold the needle with cast-on stitches in your left hand and an empty needle in your right hand. The working yarn should extend out the back. I like to hold the working yarn looped over my right index finger, draped between it and my middle finger, and looped again over my pinky finger for tension.

2. Insert the tip of the right-hand needle through the front loop of the first stitch on the left-hand needle.

3. Bring your working yarn around the left-hand needle, going clockwise, as shown.

4. Use the right needle to catch the wrapped yarn and pull it through the loop of your first cast-on stitch, transferring the new loop onto your right-hand needle and dropping the stitch off the left-hand needle. A new stitch has been made. Yay!

5. Repeat steps 2–4 to knit more stitches.

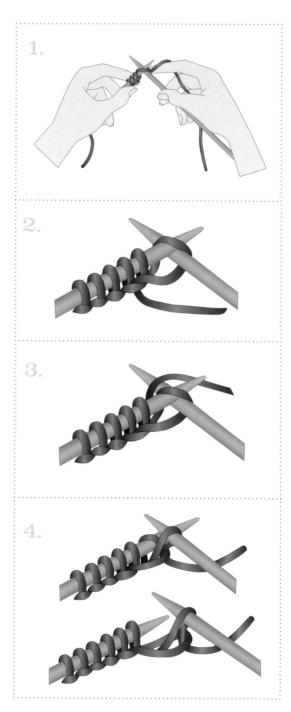

the purl stitch (p)

A purl stitch is basically the opposite of a knit stitch. It may feel a little more awkward at first, but with a little bit of practice you will have the hang of it in no time.

1. Hold the needles just as you did for a knit stitch, but this time the working yarn should extend out the front.

2. Insert the tip of the right-hand needle through the loop of the first stitch on the left-hand needle, from right to left. Bring the working yarn around the left needle, going counterclockwise, as shown.

3. Pull the right needle back through the loop, lifting the needle slightly to transfer the new loop onto the right needle and dropping the stitch from the left needle. A purl stitch is complete.

4. Repeat steps 2–3 to purl more stitches.

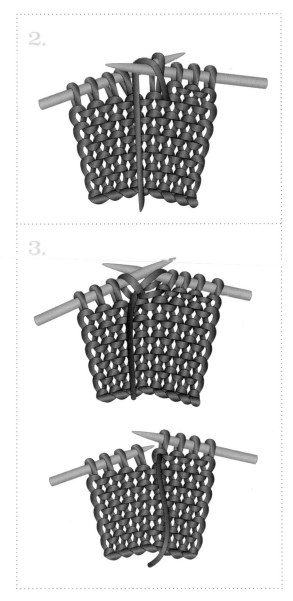

2.

3.

joining to knit in the round

To knit on circular needles, you need to "join" the two needles, so the knitted piece is in a continuous circle. This might feel a little awkward at first, but it's easy once you've tried it a few times.

1. Cast on the number of stitches needed for the pattern, just as you would on straight needles, but cast on 1 extra stitch. Make sure all the stitches are facing the same direction and none are twisted.

2. If everything looks good, bring your left-hand needle and right-hand needle to meet in the center, as if the needle were a closed circle. Your yarn tail should be on the right-hand side.

3. This is when the extra stitch comes in. Slide the extra stitch from the right-hand to the left-hand needle, then place a stitch marker on the right-hand needle. This marks the beginning of your round.

4. Knit the first two stitches on the left needle together (k2tog). This creates a stronger join and also helps hide where you began to knit in the round. Now simply continue to knit around and around! Each time you get to the stitch marker, slide it over to the other needle and keep going—this tells you you've completed one round. Told you it was easy.

RIGHT SIDE VS. WRONG SIDE

When knitting in stockinette stitch, you can tell the difference between the right and wrong side of your fabric by looking closely at each side. The "right" side of the fabric will be smooth, with little V-shaped stitches. The "wrong" side will be slightly bumpier looking, and the stitches flatter and wider. Since we will be using a circular needle throughout most of this book, you won't need to worry about the right and wrong sides of your knitted piece. The right side (or "public" side) will be on the outside; the wrong side on the inside.

increasing & decreasing

To shape a hat, you'll need to "increase," or add stitches, and "decrease," or take away stitches, to make the knitting bigger and smaller. There are many ways to increase and decrease—the patterns in this book use just a few very simple ones.

make 1 (m1)

This is a simple way to increase by 1 stitch. There are several versions of this particular stitch, but here's how I've used it in this book.

1. Use your right needle to hook under the bar between the stitch on your right-hand needle and the next stitch on your left-hand needle. Pass this loop onto your left-hand needle.

2. With your right-hand needle, knit into the *back* of this loop. You have added 1 stitch.

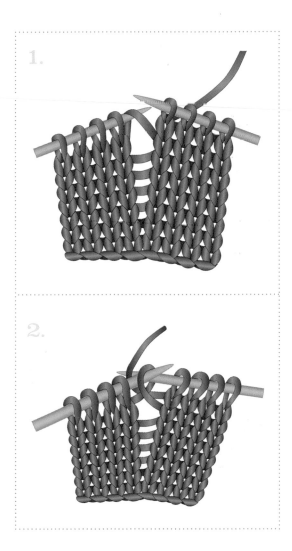

knit into front and back of same stitch (kfb)

Another simple way to increase by 1 stitch. I also use it to make bobbles.

1. Knit into the front of a stitch as normal, but don't slip the stitch off the left needle.

2. Now, *without* removing the stitch from your needle, knit into the back of the same stitch. The last bit is a little like making a purl stitch. Slip the completed stitch off the left needle.

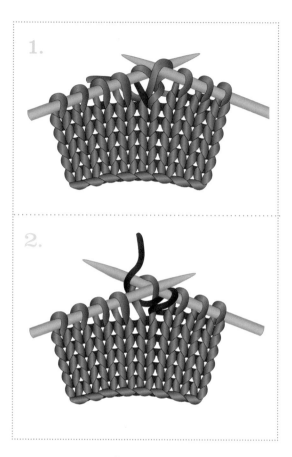

knit 2 together (k2tog)

To make this simple decrease stitch, you take 2 stitches and knit them together as one.
Insert the tip of your right-hand needle into both of the next 2 stitches on your left-hand needle. Wrap yarn as for a regular knit stitch, and knit both stitches together.

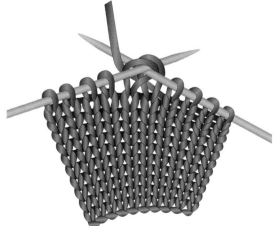

knit 3 together (k3tog)

This decrease is the same as knit 2 together, only with 3 stitches.

Insert the tip of your right-hand needle into the next 3 stitches on your left-hand needle. Wrap yarn as usual for a knit stitch and knit all 3 stitches together.

purl 2 together (p2tog)

This is a decrease where you purl 2 stitches together as if they were one.

Insert the tip of your right-hand needle into the front of the next 2 stitches. Wrap your yarn as usual for a purl stitch and purl both stitches together.

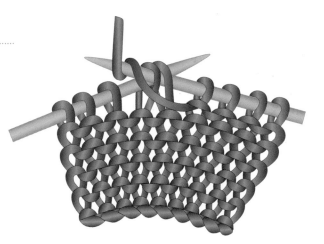

other basic techniques

slip 1 stitch (sl1)

Slipping a stitch means to move the stitch from the left needle to the right needle without knitting it.

To slip a stitch knitwise (sl1kw), insert the tip of your right-hand needle into the back of the next stitch as if you were going to knit the stitch. Without wrapping the yarn, slip the stitch from the left needle to the right needle. You have just slipped 1 stitch knitwise.

To slip a stitch purlwise (sl1pw), insert the tip of your right-hand needle into the front of the next stitch as if you were going to purl the stitch. Without wrapping the yarn, slip the stitch from the left needle to the right needle. You have just slipped 1 stitch purlwise.

sl1kw

sl1pw

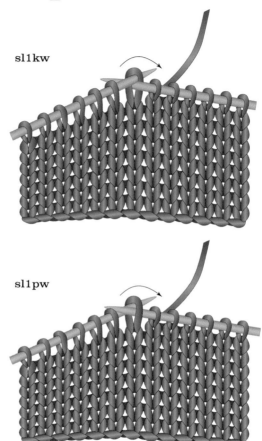

pass slipped stitch over (psso)

Passing a slipped stitch over a knitted stitch is usually part of the following instructions: slip 1, knit 1, psso, or pass the slipped stitch over the knitted stitch and off the needle. It is another way to create a decrease.

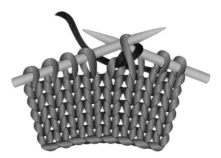

yarn over (yo)

This is simply a way to create a hole in your knitting for lace or eyelets.

Bring the working yarn around to the front of your needle, loop it over the needle, then knit the next stitch.

joining a new color or new ball of yarn

When it comes time to change color, or when you need to attach a new ball of yarn because the old one has run out, just cut your working yarn at the beginning of a row, leaving a 6-inch-long (15cm) tail. There are two ways to attach the new yarn:

Tie the new color onto the old tail with a loose knot at the end of a row, as shown at right.

Start your next stitch, wrapping with both your old yarn tail *and* the new yarn, and pull both through. Then just drop your old yarn and continue knitting or purling as usual with your new yarn, as shown below right.

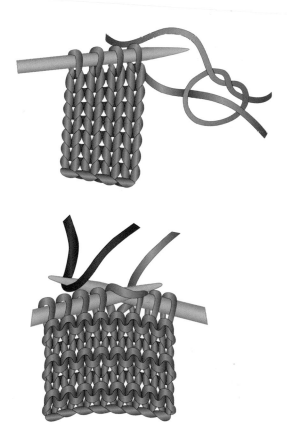

pick up stitches and knit

Sometimes you need to create new stitches along the edge of a finished piece of knitting, usually when you want to make an edging. Sometimes you will pick up stitches horizontally from the beginning or end of the knitting and sometimes you will pick up stitches vertically along the edge of the rows. Here's how to do it.

To pick up stitches horizontally:

1. With the right side of the work facing you, insert the needle into the edge under both loops as if you were going to knit, and wrap the yarn around the needle.

2. Bring the needle through to the front to create a loop. Continue along the edge, picking up loops until you have all the loops on the needle and are ready to knit a row.

To pick up stitches vertically:

1. With the right side of the work facing you, insert the needle into the edge of the first row under both loops as if you were going to knit, and wrap the yarn around the needle.

2. Bring the needle through to the front to create a loop. Continue along the edge, evenly picking up the number of stitches indicated in the pattern until you have all the loops on the needle and are ready to knit a row.

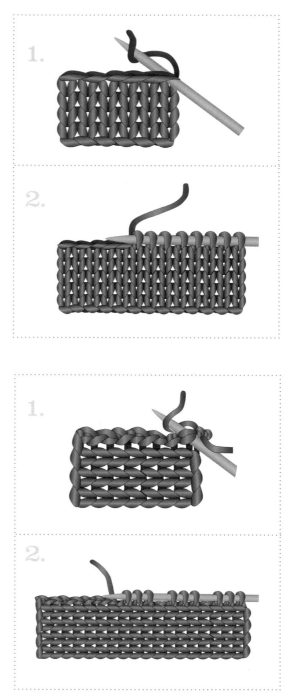

changing to DPNs

You want to start knitting with double-pointed needles as soon as you have too few stitches to continue comfortably with a circular needle. I like to use a set of four DPNs, with the stitches spread over three of the needles and using the fourth needle to knit with.

To transfer stitches, I find it easiest to simply begin knitting the first decreasing round right onto the DPNs. For most of the hats in this book, with your first needle, you will knit 6 stitches straight onto the first DPN, then k2tg straight onto the DPN. Do this twice more. Then repeat with your second DPN, and your third until all of the stitches have been transferred.

Working with DPNs may feel a little awkward at first. Your stitches won't fall off the needles, so to make things easier, hold onto only the two needles you are working with at any one time. Let the other two needles hang down. Once all the stitches are on the DPNs, simply continue to knit each round as you would on your circular needle. Slip a marker into the first stitch of a round to remind you which row you are up to.

KNITTING TERMS

Here are two terms you will see often in knitting; they describe types of fabric or texture that you can create with knit and purl stitches. They are created differently depending on whether you are knitting back and forth in rows or knitting in the round.

GARTER STITCH
• **Knitting back and forth:** You knit every row.

• **Knitting in the round:** You alternate knit and purl rounds.

STOCKINETTE STITCH
• **Knitting back and forth:** You alternate rows of knit and purl.

• **Knitting in the round:** You knit every round.

binding off (bo)

When you've finished most knitting, you need to secure the last row of stitches, so they don't come unraveled. In only a few of my hats do you need to bind off remaining stitches, but you do have to know how to do it!

1. Knit the first 2 stitches of your last row.

2. With tip of your left-hand needle, lift the rightmost stitch over the second stitch on your right-hand needle, as shown, and drop it off the needle.

3. Knit 1 more stitch as usual, then repeat step 2.

4. Continue on in this manner until all stitches have been bound off.

5. When you're finished, cut your working yarn, leaving a 6-inch (15cm) tail. Loosen the last loop on your needle and carefully slide it off. Thread the tail through the loop and pull to tighten.

three-needle bind-off

I absolutely hate joining seams together. I find them bulky and time-consuming. I use the three-needle bind-off technique for seams because it is fast, easy once you know how to do it, and creates a nice clean seam that looks both neat and professional. This is very similar to a normal bind-off, only you join together one stitch from each needle as you bind off.

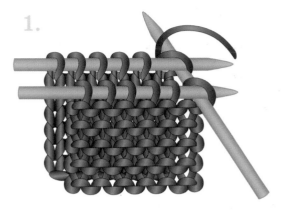

1. Divide the remaining stitches evenly onto two DPNs and turn the work so the right side is on the inside. Insert the tip of a third DPN into the front of the first stitch on *each* needle. Knit these 2 stitches together. Repeat for the second stitch on both needles.

2. With your left-hand DPN, lift the first stitch over the second stitch on the working DPN and drop it off. Repeat until all stitches have been bound off.

weaving in yarn ends

You need to weave the yarn ends (from starting and finishing, color changes or ball changes) into the knitting to finish your piece and tidy things up. Weaving in the ends also stops all of your hard work from coming unraveled.

Thread the yarn end onto a yarn needle (or a blunt tapestry needle), and bring the needle under several bars of stitches on the wrong side, or inside, of the knitted piece, "weaving" the yarn end through.

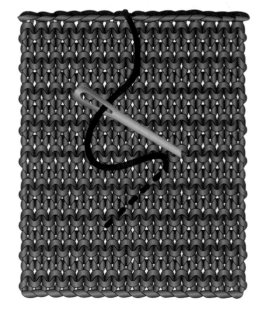

cute endings

pompoms

I like to use a plastic pompom creator, available at any craft store. If you don't have one of these, you can use cardboard circles.

1. Cut two cardboard circles the size you want the pompom to be and then cut a hole in the center of each one. Hold the circles together and wrap yarn around the circles. The more yarn you wrap, the fuller your pompom will be.

2. Cut the yarn around the edge between the circles. Before removing the yarn, tie a length of yarn tightly around the middle of the yarn bundle between the two pieces of cardboard. Remove the cardboard, fluff up the pompom, and trim the yarn ends, if you like.

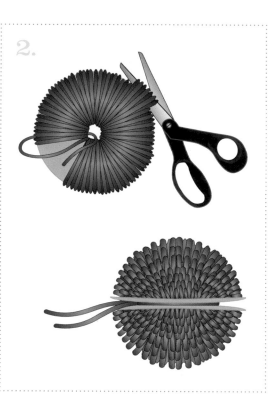

i-cord

Use DPNs to create what Elizabeth Zimmerman calls "idiot cord"—a small tube used for ties or for the tops on many hats (see page 60).

Cast 2–4 stitches on your DPN, knit 1 row. Keeping the DPN in the same hand and without turning it, slide the stitches to the other end of the needle and knit them again, pulling the working yarn tight across the back as you knit. Continue knitting like this, gently pulling down on the cord as it is being formed, until the i-cord is as long as the pattern specifies.

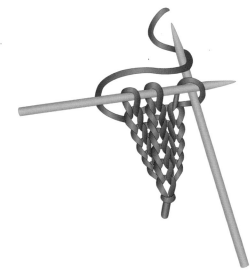

tassels

Tassels, groups of long yarn tied at the top, make a nice finish on a baby hat.

1. Cut out a piece of stiff cardboard to the length you want the tassel.

2. Wrap yarn around the cardboard lengthways. I wrap 20–30 times for a normal-sized tassel, more or less for a fuller or thinner one.

3. With the yarn still wrapped around the card, take a strand of yarn and slide it under all of the strands of yarn on the cardboard. Tie a knot at the top to secure the tassel, cut the ends of yarn at the bottom. Carefully slide the yarn off the cardboard.

4. Take another strand of yarn and wrap it around the yarn about half an inch from the top of the tassel and knot tightly. Pull the ends to the inside of the tassel with a yarn needle.

3.

4.

the beanies

What better way to learn to knit than by creating an adorable little cap for a tiny person in your life? Most of these hats are very easy—perfect for practicing your skills or brushing up on technique. Some are cute and quirky with bold stripes, chunky pompoms, and funky loops—just right for expressing a sense of fun. Some are sweet and whimsical for the perfect dose of cute. And all are guaranteed to elicit an "awwww" from passers-by.

simple roll-brimmed hat

Most beginner knitting books have you start with a simple (and boring) garter-stitch scarf. I think you will learn more and have a lot more fun if you start with this roll-brimmed hat. It requires only basic skills, and the reward for your efforts is a cute little hat. The rolled brim also means it will fit a variety of heads, so there is no need to stress about size.

SKILLS REQUIRED
Long-tail cast-on, knit 2 together (k2tog), pompoms

YOU WILL NEED
- Size 9 (5.5mm) 12- or 16-inch circular needles and set of 4 or 5 double-pointed needles
- Mission Falls 1824 Wool (100% Merino superwash wool; 1¾ oz/50g/85 yards), 1 ball in Sprout 0531 (A)
- Small amount of yarn in contrasting color (B)
- Stitch marker
- Yarn needle

GAUGE
16 stitches and 26 rounds = 4 inches

SIZES
0–6 months (6–12 months, 1–2 years, 2 years and up)

FINISHED CIRCUMFERENCE
12 (14, 16, 18) inches

pattern

With A, cast on 48 (56, 64, 72) stitches, place marker, and slip a stitch marker onto your RH needle, or into the first stitch, to mark the beginning of the round. (You will do this with every pattern to see where the start and finish of a round of knitting is.) Join to begin knitting in the round.

TIP: To make joining to knit in the round easier, cast on 1 extra stitch and knit the extra stitch together with the first stitch from the LH needle. See page 28.

Work in stockinette (knit every round) for 5 (5½, 6, 6½) inches from cast-on edge. Do not measure the length from the brim, or your hat will be too long. As you knit, you will find that the brim rolls up naturally by itself.

DECREASING
Round 1: Knit 6, k2tog. Repeat to end of round.

Round 2: Knit.

Round 3: Knit 5, k2tog. Repeat to end of round.

Round 4: Knit.

Round 5: Knit 4, k2tog. Repeat to end of round.

Round 6: Knit.

TIP: Switch to the DPNs when there are too few stitches to continue knitting comfortably on the circular needle.

Round 7: Knit 3, k2tog. Repeat to end of round.

Round 8: Knit.

Round 9: Knit 2, k2tog. Repeat to end of round.

Round 10: Knit.

Round 11: Knit 1, k2tog. Repeat to end of round.

Round 12: K2tog. Repeat to end of round.

Cut yarn, leaving a 6-inch tail. Using a yarn needle, finish off the top of the hat by threading the tail through the remaining stitches. Thread end through the hole at top of the hat, turn the hat inside out, and pull tightly to close.

TIP: Close the circle at the top by threading the tail through the first stitch twice, once in the beginning, and once after all stitches have been removed from the needle.

finishing

To add some extra cuteness, I've finished off the hat with two braided cords and some pompoms. Cut two lengths of A and four lengths of B twice the length of desired braid. Divide into two sets. Knot threads of each set together at one end and braid the lengths together. With B, create two 2½-inch pompoms (see page 38), trimming as necessary, and attach to braid. Attach opposite end of braids to top of hat. I pull the braid slightly inside the join at the top of the hat and then sew it on the inside. Weave in all ends to finish.

Pompoms on braided cords add just the right note to this simple roll-brimmed hat.

special day silk hat

When I created this pattern, I had in mind something sweet and decidedly feminine. I wanted it to look just as good with everyday clothes as it does with special occasion dresses, so you could get more than just one use out of it before tucking it away as an heirloom treasure. The ruffled brim and woven-in ribbon lend an air of girlishness, and the cotton-and-silk blend yarn has a gentle sheen, making it the perfect special day hat. I used a shimmery gauze ribbon, but it would look equally sweet with plain grosgrain ribbon or even ribbon in bright colors or with polka dots!

SKILLS REQUIRED
Long-tail cast-on, knit 3 together (k3tog), knit 2 together (k2tog), yarn over (yo)

YOU WILL NEED
- Size 7 (4.5mm) 12- or 16-inch circular and set of 4 or 5 double-pointed needles
- Cascade Pima Silk (85% Peruvian pima cotton, 15% silk; 1¾ oz/50g/109 yards), 1 skein in 5136 pink
- One yard of ¾-inch-wide gauze ribbon in complementary shade
- Stitch marker
- Yarn needle

GAUGE
20 stitches and 26 rounds = 4 inches

SIZES
0–6 months (6–12 months, 1–2 years, 2 years and up)

FINISHED CIRCUMFERENCE
12¾ (14½, 16, 17½) inches

pattern

Cast on 192 (216, 240, 264) stitches, place marker, and join to begin knitting in the round. (The large number of stitches is required to form the ruffle and will decrease on the next round.)

Round 1: Knit all stitches, keeping this first round of stitches fairly loose to make the next round easier.

Round 2: K3tog. Repeat to end of round—64 (72, 80, 88) stitches remain.

Work in stockinette, knitting all stitches, for ½ inch.

Eyelet round: Yo, k2tog, yo, k2tog, knit 4. Repeat to end of round.

Continue in stockinette, knitting all stitches, until piece measures 5½ (6, 6½, 7) inches from the cast-on edge.

DECREASING

Round 1: Knit 6, k2tog. Repeat to end of round.

Round 2 and all even-numbered rounds through round 10: Knit.

Round 3: Knit 5, k2tog. Repeat to end of round.

Round 5: Knit 4, k2tog. Repeat to end of round.

Round 7: Knit 3, k2tog. Repeat to end of round.

Round 9: Knit 2, k2tog. Repeat to end of round.

Round 11: Knit 1, k2tog. Repeat to end of round.

Round 12: K2tog. Repeat to end of round.

Snip yarn, leaving a 6-inch tail, and using a yarn needle thread tail through remaining stitches. Pass tail through hole at center of hat and pull tightly to close. Weave in all ends.

finishing

Thread length of ribbon through eyelets, allowing several inches extra for give when the hat stretches. Tie the ends of ribbon in a loopy bow. Cut excess ribbon.

pompom bear

Need a last-minute gift? This hat is the perfect thing to knit—it's a quick, fun to make, and worked in simple garter stitch. There is no shaping required; the hat is simply a square. The pompoms look like little ears and give the hat great teddy-bear appeal.

SKILLS REQUIRED
Long-tail cast-on, 3-needle bind-off, pompoms

YOU WILL NEED
- Size 9 (5.5mm) 12- or 16-inch circular needles and set of 4 or 5 double-pointed needles
- Malabrigo Worsted Hand-Dyed Merino (100% merino wool; 3½ oz/100g/215 yards), 1 skein in Autumn Forest 224
- Stitch marker
- Yarn needle

GAUGE
16 stitches and 20 rounds = 4 inches in garter stitch

SIZES
0–6 months (6–12 months, 1–2 years, 2 years and up)

FINISHED CIRCUMFERENCE
14 (16, 18, 20) inches

pattern

Cast on 56 (64, 72, 80) stitches, place marker, and join to begin knitting in the round.

Round 1: Knit 2, purl 2. Continue to end of round. Repeat round 1 five more times.

Round 2: Purl.

Round 3: Knit.

Repeat rounds 2 and 3 until hat measures 6 (6½, 7, 7½) inches from cast-on edge.

Turn hat inside out and divide remaining stitches evenly over two DPNs. Bind off all stitches using the 3-needle bind-off technique (see page 37).

TIP: If you are using a circular needle with a soft and flexible cord, you can bypass moving the stitches onto DPNs. Simply bend the cord in half, divide stitches as you would for DPNs, and bind off with a DPN.

finishing

Make two small pompoms (see page 38) and attach to top points of the hat. Weave in all ends to finish.

flowered miss

This is a really quick to knit, super easy hat with a simple ribbing. The "wow" factor comes from the embellishment that you add at the end.

SKILLS REQUIRED
Long-tail cast-on, knit 2 together (k2tog)

YOU WILL NEED
- Size 9 (5.5 mm) 12- or 16-inch circular needles and set of 4 or 5 double-pointed needles
  Cascade Yarns Cash Vero (55% merino extra fine wool, 33% microfiber, 12% cashmere; 1¾ oz/50g/98 yards), 1 skein in #006
- Stitch marker
- Yarn needle
- Tulle, 6 by 18 inches (optional)
- 1-inch button (optional; skip for younger babies)

GAUGE
16 stitches and 24 rounds = 4 inches

SIZES
0–6 months (6–12 months, 1–2 years, 2 years and up)

FINISHED CIRCUMFERENCE
12 (14, 16, 18) inches

pattern

Cast on 48 (56, 64, 72) stitches, place marker, and join to begin knitting in the round.

Round 1: Knit 2, purl 2. Repeat to end of round.

Repeat round 1 five more times (6 rounds total).

Work in stockinette stitch (knit every round) until piece measures 5 (5½, 6, 6½) inches from the cast-on edge.

DECREASING
Round 1: Knit 6, k2tog. Repeat to end of round.

Round 2 and all even-numbered rounds through round 10: Knit.

Round 3: Knit 5, k2tog. Repeat to end of round.

Round 5: Knit 4, k2tog. Repeat to end of round.

Round 7: Knit 3, k2tog. Repeat to end of round.

Round 9: Knit 2, k2tog. Repeat to end of round.

Round 11: Knit 1, k2tog. Repeat to end of round.

Round 12: K2tog. Repeat to end of round.

Cut yarn, leaving a 6-inch tail. Using yarn needle, thread tail through remaining stitches and pull tight to secure. Weave in all ends to finish.

finishing

For the flower decoration, I bought tulle at my local craft shop, gathered one edge with long running stitches, and pulled it gently into a circle, then sewed it to the side of the hat and added a button. (For safety reasons, it's best to leave the button off for younger babies.)

pinky snuggles

Yarn from Blue Sky Alpacas is wonderful! Their worsted hand-dyed merino/alpaca blend is irresistibly soft and snuggly and a delight to work with. The hand-dying process gives the yarn subtle yet gorgeous color variations. To add interest to this hat, I used a novelty yarn with fun colors and extra tufts of yarn for the stripes and the sprout at the top.

SKILLS REQUIRED

Long-tail cast-on, knit 2 together (k2tog), joining new color, pompoms

YOU WILL NEED

- Size 9 (5.5mm) 12- or 16-inch circular needles and set of 4 or 5 double-pointed needles
- Blue Sky Alpacas Worsted Hand Dyes (50% alpaca, 50% merino; 3½ oz/100g/ 100 yards), 1 skein in 2018 Strawberry (A)
- Approximately ¼ skein any worsted weight "novelty" yarn. I used Filati Bertagna Primitivo (60% merino wool, 32% acrylic, 8% nylon; 1¾ oz/50g/55 yards) in #65 pink/orange/brown (B).
- Stitch marker
- Yarn needle

GAUGE

16 stitches and 24 rounds = 4 inches in yarn A

SIZES

0–6 months (6–12 months, 1–2 years, 2 years and up)

FINISHED CIRCUMFERENCE

12 (14, 16, 18) inches

pattern

With A, cast on 48 (56, 64, 72) stitches, place marker, and join to begin knitting in the round. Work in stockinette, knitting all stitches, until piece measures 2 inches from the cast-on edge. Change to B.

Round 1: Purl.

Round 2: Purl.

Change back to A. Work in stockinette, knitting all stitches, for 1 inch.

Change to B.

Round 1: Purl.

Round 2: Purl.

Change back to A and work in stockinette until piece measures 5 (5½, 6, 6½) inches from the cast-on edge.

DECREASING

Round 1: Knit 6, k2tog. Repeat to end of round.

Round 2 and all even-numbered rounds through round 10: Knit.

Round 3: Knit 5, k2tog. Repeat to end of round.

Round 5: Knit 4, k2tog. Repeat to end of round.

Round 7: Knit 3, k2tog. Repeat to end of round.

Round 9: Knit 2, k2tog. Repeat to end of round.

Round 11: Knit 1, k2tog. Repeat to end of round.

Round 12: K2tog. Repeat to end of round.

Snip yarn, leaving a 6-inch tail, and using yarn needle thread through remaining stitches. Pass through hole at center of the hat and pull tightly to close.

finishing

Create a sprout—a very loose pompom (see page 38)—for the top using B and wrapping the yarn 20 times around your palm. Use A to tie the pompom and secure it to the top of the hat. Weave in the ends.

flour sack

I call this hat the Flour Sack because it reminds me of the burlap flour sacks of olden days with its rustic texture and little tied corners. The construction is simple with no shaping, so it's perfect for beginning knitters. You tie the corners of the hat after you bind off.

SKILLS REQUIRED
Long-tail cast-on, knit 2 together (k2tog), joining new color, 3-needle bind-off

YOU WILL NEED
- Size 7 (4.5mm) 12- or 16-inch circular needles and set of 4 or 5 double-pointed needles
- Mission Falls 1824 Cotton (100% cotton; 1¾ oz/50g/85 yards), 1 skein each of Ivory 102 (A) and Pebble 103 (B)
- Stitch marker
- Yarn needle

GAUGE
20 stitches and 26 rounds = 4 inches in Stockinette

SIZES
0–6 months (6–12 months, 1–2 years, 2 years and up)

FINISHED CIRCUMFERENCE
11¼ (12¾, 14½, 16) inches

pattern

With A, cast on 56 (64, 72, 80) stitches, place marker, and join to begin knitting in the round.

Round 1: Knit 1, purl 1. Repeat to end of round.

Repeat above round until piece measures 1½ (2, 2½, 2½) inches. Break yarn.

Change to B.

Work in stockinette (knit all stitches) for 4 (4½, 5, 6) inches.

Carefully turn hat inside out and divide stitches evenly between two DPNs. Bind off all stitches using the 3-needle bind-off technique (see page 37). Weave in all ends and turn the hat right-side out.

finishing

Cut two 6-inch lengths of B. Gather the top corners of the hat, using the tip of your finger to create a "fold" in the middle of each. Tie a knot around each corner with a length of yarn and tie in a bow. Trim ends. Turn up brim to finish.

long-tail hat

When a baby wears this hat, the long "tail" (aka, i-cord) will swish from side to side, just like the tail of a cute baby elephant. Use any two colors that grab you—see page 40 for the same hat knit in light aqua and gray.

pattern

With A, cast on 48 (56, 64, 72) stitches, place marker, and join to begin knitting in the round.

Work in stockinette (knit every round) until piece measures 1½ (1½, 2, 2) inches from the cast-on edge. Note: Stockinette edge will curl, so unroll for an accurate measurement.

Change to B.

Continue in stockinette stitch until piece measures 5 (5½, 6, 6½) inches from the cast-on edge.

DECREASING

Round 1: Knit 6, k2tog. Repeat to end of round.

Round 2: Knit.

Round 3: Knit 5, k2tog. Repeat to end of round.

Round 4: Knit.

Round 5: Knit 4, k2tog. Repeat to end of round.

Round 6: Knit.

Round 7: Knit 3, k2tog. Repeat to end of round.

Rounds 8–13: Knit.

Round 14: Knit 2, k2tog. Repeat to end of round.

Rounds 15–19: Knit.

Round 20: Knit 1, k2tog. Repeat to end of round.

Change to A.

Rounds 22–25: Knit.

Round 26: K2tog. Repeat to end of round.

Continue to k2tog until only 4 stitches remain.

Transfer these 4 stitches onto a single DPN and work i-cord (see page 38) for 4–5 inches. Bind off all stitches.

finishing

With B, create a small tassel (see page 39) and attach it to the end of the i-cord. Wrap a length of B around the base several times. Weave in all ends to finish.

SKILLS REQUIRED
Long-tail cast-on, knit 2 together (k2tog),
joining new color, i-cord, tassels

YOU WILL NEED
- Size 9 (5.5mm) 12- or 16-inch circular
  needles and set of 4 or 5 double-pointed
  needles
- Mission Falls 1824 Wool (100% Merino
  superwash wool; 1¾ oz/50g/85 yards),
  1 ball each of Rhubarb 534 (A) and
  Squash 533 (B)
- Stitch marker
- Yarn needle

GAUGE
16 stitches = 4 inches

SIZES
0–6 months (6–12 months, 1–2 years,
2 years and up)

FINISHED CIRCUMFERENCE
14 (16, 18, 20) inches

accordion hat

I first made this hat in neutral colors, and the alternating knit and purl
ridges made me think of the way an accordion folds in on itself and then
stretches back out again. While the neutrals were nice, I really wanted
this hat to stand out, so I chose bright pink and orange—and the contrast
between these vivid colors really plays up the hat's resemblance to
an accordion.

pattern

With A, cast on 56 (64, 72, 80) stitches, place marker, and join to begin knitting in the round.

Work in stockinette (knit every round) for 1 inch from cast-on edge.

Change to B.

Round 1: Knit.

Rounds 2–5: Purl.

Change to A.

Rounds 6–9: Knit.

Repeat rounds 1 through 9 as above until (unstretched) hat measures 5 (5½, 6, 6½) inches from cast-on edge, ending with a knit row in A.

DECREASING

Still using A,

Round 1: Knit 6, k2tog. Repeat to end of round.

Round 2 and all even-numbered rounds through round 10: Knit.

Round 3: Knit 5, k2tog. Repeat to end of round.

Round 5: Knit 4, k2tog. Repeat to end of round.

Round 7: Knit 3, k2tog. Repeat to end of round.

Round 9: Knit 2, k2tog. Repeat to end of round.

Round 11: Knit 1, k2tog. Repeat to end of round.

Round 12: K2tog. Repeat to end of round.

Continue to k2tog until only 4 stitches remain.

Transfer remaining 4 stitches to a single DPN and work i-cord (see page 38) for ½ inch. Bind off. Cut yarn and weave in ends.

finishing

Make small, short tassel with B (see page 39) and attach to top of i-cord. Wrap length of yarn around base of tassel and secure.

The Accordion Hat is as cute from the back as it is from the front, with a short tassel that stands straight up.

alien spaceship

When I started this hat, I wanted something a bit quirky with lots of bobbles in bright colors. When my two older kids saw this hat on their little sister, they immediately decided that an alien spaceship had taken up residence on her head, and so I had my hat name!

SKILLS REQUIRED

Long-tail cast-on, knit 2 together (k2tog), joining new color, make bobbles (mb), tassels

YOU WILL NEED

- Size 9 (5.5mm) 12- or 16-inch circular and set of 4 or 5 double-pointed needles
- Brown Sheep Lamb's Pride Worsted (85% wool, 15% mohair; 4 oz/113g/190 yards), 1 skein each of M120 Limeade (A), M078 Aztec Turquoise (B), M081 Red Baron (C), and M110 Orange You Glad (D)
- Stitch marker
- Yarn needle

GAUGE

16 stitches and 26 rounds = 4 inches

SIZES

0–6 months (6–12 months, 1–2 years, 2 years and up)

FINISHED CIRCUMFERENCE

14 (16, 18, 20) inches

pattern

With A, cast on 56 (64, 72, 80) stitches, place marker, and join to begin knitting in the round.

Work in stockinette (knit every round) until piece measures 2 (2½, 2½, 2½) inches from the cast-on edge.

Round 1: Knit 7 with A, mb of 5 stitches (see page 66) with B. Repeat to end of round.

TIP: When making bobbles, strand the second color (the working yarn for bobbles) *very* loosely along the back of the knitted piece, knitting the working yarn in every few stitches.

Rounds 2–4: With A, knit.

Round 5: Knit 3 with A, mb with C, *knit 7, mb*. Repeat from * to * until end of round.

Rounds 6–8: Knit with A.

Round 9: Knit 7 with A, mb with D. Repeat to end of round.

With A, continue in stockinette until piece measures 5 (5½, 6, 6½) inches from cast-on edge.

DECREASING

Round 1: Knit 6, k2tog. Repeat to end of round.

Round 2 and all even-numbered rounds through round 10: Knit.

Round 3: Knit 5, k2tog. Repeat to end of round.

Round 5: Knit 4, k2tog. Repeat to end of round.

Round 7: Knit 3, k2tog. Repeat to end of round.

Round 9: Knit 2, k2tog. Repeat to end of round.

Round 11: Knit 1, k2tog. Repeat to end of round.

Round 12: K2tog. Repeat to end of round.

Continue knitting the remaining stitches for 1 inch.

Cut yarn, leaving a 6-inch tail, and using a yarn needle thread tail through stitches, pulling tightly to close.

finishing

With B, make a 1-inch tassel (see page 39) and attach to top point of hat's "stalk." Wrap a length of B around the base of tassel to make it stand up straight. Weave in all ends.

MAKE BOBBLE (mb)

Bobbles are fat little bumps in the knitting made by working several stitches into one stitch. (See Knit into Front and Back of Same Stitch, page 30.) These bobbles are made with just 5 stitches, but you can make yours smaller or larger. Experiment to see what you like. You can also make the bobbles in the same color as the hat for a completely different look.

1. Cast on 1 stitch.

2. Knit into the front, back, front, back, front, of the same stitch (5 times total). You will have 5 stitches on your right-hand needle.

3. Purl all stitches.

4. Knit all stitches. Without turning the work, pass the second, third, and fourth stitches over the first stitch separately until only that one stitch remains.

5. Pass this stitch back to your left-hand needle and knit it again. Bobble created.

euro bébé

"Fair Isle" is the name given to this type of knitting using two or more colors of yarn in the same row; it is named after an island in Scotland famous for its patterned sweaters. The technique used is called "stranding" to describe how you carry the yarn. This pattern is relatively simple—just be sure to keep your stitches nice and loose so the fabric doesn't bunch and pucker.

SKILLS REQUIRED
Long-tail cast on, knit 2 together (k2tog), joining new color, stranded knitting, i-cord

YOU WILL NEED
- Size 7 (4.5mm) 12- or 16-inch circular and set of 4 or 5 double-pointed needles
- Cascade 220 Wool (100% Peruvian Highland wool; 3½ oz/100g/220 yards), 1 skein each in Cherry 2426 (A), Cotton Candy 9478 (B), Burnt Orange 7824 (C)
- Stitch marker
- Yarn needle

GAUGE
20 stitches and 28 rounds = 4 inches

SIZES
0–6 months (6–12 months, 1–2 years, 2 years and up)

FINISHED CIRCUMFERENCE
12¾ (14½, 16, 17½) inches

pattern

With A, cast on 64 (72, 80, 88) stitches, place marker, and join to begin knitting in the round.

Round 1: Knit 1, purl 1. Continue to end of round.

Rounds 2–4: Repeat round 1.

Change to B.

Rounds 5–7: Knit.

Round 8: Knit 1 in C, knit 1 in B. Repeat to end of round.

Round 9: With B, knit all stitches.

Round 10: Knit 2 in B, knit 1 in C. Repeat to end of round.

Round 11: Knit 1 in B, knit 1 in C. Repeat to end of round.

Round 12: Repeat round 10.

Round 13: Knit all stitches in B.

Repeat rounds 8–13 once more.

Round 14: Knit 1 C, knit 1 B. Repeat to end of round.

Round 15: Knit all stitches in B.

Repeat round 15 for 2 (3, 3, 4) more rounds.

Round 16: Change to A. Knit all stitches.

Round 17: Purl.

Round 18: Change to C. Knit all stitches.

Repeat round 18 for 4 (5, 5, 6) more rounds.

Round 19: Change to A. Knit all stitches.

Round 20: Purl.

Round 21: Change to C. Knit all stitches.

Repeat round 21 for 4 (5, 5, 6) more rounds.

Round 22: Change to A. Knit.

Round 23: Purl.

DECREASING

While decreasing, work stripe pattern as follows:

Knit 3 rounds in B, knit 3 rounds in C.

Round 1: Knit 6, k2tog. Repeat to end of round.

Round 2: Knit.

Round 3: Knit.

Round 4: Knit 5, k2tog. Repeat to end of round.

Round 5: Knit.

Round 6: Knit 4, k2tog. Repeat to end of round.

Round 7: Knit.

Round 8: Knit 3, k2tog. Repeat to end of round.

Rounds 9–15: Knit.

Round 16: Knit 2, k2tog. Repeat to end of round.

Continue in B to end.

Rounds 17–22: Knit.

Round 23: Knit 1, k2tog. Repeat to end of round.

Rounds 24–27: Knit.

Round 28: K2tog. Repeat to end of round.

Round 29: K2tog, repeating until only 4 stitches remain.

Transfer remaining 4 stitches onto a double-pointed needle. Work i-cord (see page 38) for 4 inches. Bind off remaining stitches and weave in ends.

finishing

Make a knot in the i-cord to finish.

STRANDED KNITTING

Stranded knitting is a technique used for "Fair Isle" knitting, a traditional style that uses two or more colors of yarn at the same time to create a pattern. The unused yarn is held loosely at the back of the work, stranded (or "floating") behind the stitches, as you alternate between each color. Try holding one color in each hand, if that feels comfortable, or you can pick up and drop the unused color with your right hand as you need it. Remember to keep your gauge quite loose when knitting this way because it is very easy to strand the yarn too tightly, causing the work to pucker.

Secure the floating yarn every few stitches by wrapping the working yarn around the floating yarn.

The second color yarn is stranded or "floats" behind the stitches.

loopy pixie

Tiny little earflaps, a funky pointed top with a little loopy curl, and beautifully textured yarn all make this one gorgeous cap. The pointed shape reminds me of the little caps worn by pixies and elves in illustrations from old fairytale storybooks.

pattern

EARFLAPS (make 2)

Using DPNs, cast on 3 stitches.

Row 1 and all odd-numbered rows through row 13: Knit.

Row 2: Kfb, knit 1, kfb.

Row 4: Kfb, knit 3, kfb.

Row 6: Kfb, knit 5, kfb.

Row 8: Kfb, knit 7, kfb.

Row 10: Kfb, knit 9, kfb.

Row 12: Kfb, knit 11, kfb (15 stitches).

Row 14: Knit.

Cut working yarn and set flap aside.

HAT

Cast on 56 (64, 72, 80) stitches.

Round 1: Knit 5 (7, 9, 11), then using 3-needle bind-off technique, join across first earflap, knit 16 (20, 24, 28), join across second earflap, knit 5 (7, 9, 11).

Round 2: Purl.

Round 3: Knit.

Round 4: Purl.

Change to stockinette (knit every round) until 3 (3½, 4, 4½) inches from cast-on edge. Do not include earflaps in measurement.

DECREASING

Round 1: Knit 12 (14, 16, 18), k2tog. Repeat to end of round.

Round 2 and all even-numbered rounds through round 16: Knit.

Round 3: Knit 11 (13, 15, 17), k2tog. Repeat to end of round.

Round 5: Knit 10 (12, 14, 16), k2tog. Repeat to end of round.

Round 7: Knit 9 (11, 13, 15), k2tog. Repeat to end of round.

Round 9: Knit 8 (10, 12, 14), k2tog. Repeat to end of round.

Round 11: Knit 7 (9, 11, 13), k2tog. Repeat to end of round.

Round 13: Knit 6 (8, 10, 12), k2tog. Repeat to end of round.

Round 15: Knit 5 (7, 9, 11), k2tog. Repeat to end of round.

Round 17: Knit 4 (6, 8, 10), k2tog. Repeat to end of round.

Rounds 18–19: Knit.

Round 20: Knit 3 (5, 7, 9), k2tog. Repeat to end of round.

Round 21–22: Knit.

Round 23: Knit 2 (4, 6, 8), k2tog. Repeat to end of round.

Round 24–25: Knit.

Round 26: Knit 1 (3, 5, 7), k2tog. Repeat to end of round. Size 0–6 months, skip to round 31.

Round 27: Knit.

Round 28: Knit _ (2, 4, 6), k2tog. Repeat to end of round. Size 6–12 months, skip to round 31.

Round 29: Knit.

Round 30: Knit _ (_, 3, 5), k2tog. Repeat to end of round.

Round 31–32: Knit.

Round 33: K2tog. Repeat to end of round.

Continue to k2tog until only 4 stitches remain. Place remaining 4 stitches on a single DPN. Knit i-cord (see page 38) for 4½ inches. Cut yarn and using a yarn needle, draw through stitches.

finishing

With yarn and a tapestry needle, sew cord to form a loop at top of hat as pictured in photograph. Weave in all ends to finish.

bright beret

I just love floppy berets on babies. There's something about the oversize look that makes me happy. This beret has an easy-to-follow eyelet pattern and is finished with the teeniest of pompoms at the top. Make it in the bright colors shown, or try it in earthy naturals or baby blues.

SKILLS REQUIRED

Long-tail cast-on, joining new color, yarn over (yo), knit 2 together (k2tog), make 1 (m1), pompoms

YOU WILL NEED

- Size 9 (5.5mm) 12- or 16-inch circular needles and set of 4 or 5 double-pointed needles
- Malabrigo Worsted Hand-Dyed Merino (100% merino wool; 3½ oz/100g/215 yards), 1 skein each in Strawberry Fields 503 (A) and Moss 505 (B)
- Stitch marker
- Yarn needle

GAUGE

16 stitches and 28 rounds = 4 inches

SIZES

0–6 months (6–12 months, 1–2 years, 2 years and up)

FINISHED CIRCUMFERENCE

12 (14, 16, 18) inches

pattern

With A, cast on 48 (56, 64, 72) stitches, place marker, and join to begin knitting in the round.

Round 1: Knit 1, purl 1. Continue to end of round.

Repeat round 1 three more times.

Change to B.

Round 1: Purl.

Round 2: Knit.

Round 3: Knit.

Round 4: Knit.

Round 5: Purl.

Round 6: Purl.

Round 7: Knit.

Round 8: Yo, k2tog. Repeat to end of round.

Round 9: Knit.

Round 10: Purl.

Round 11: Purl.

Round 12: Knit 4, m1. Repeat to end of round.

Round 13: Yo, k2tog. Repeat to end of round.

Round 14: Knit.

Round 15: Purl.

Round 16: Purl.

Round 17: Knit 5, m1. Repeat to end of round.

Change to A.

baby beanies

Work in stockinette (knit every round) for 1 (1½, 2, 2½) more inch(es).

DECREASING

Round 1: Knit 10 (12, 14, 16), k2tog. Repeat to end of round.

Round 2: Knit 9 (11, 13, 15), k2tog. Repeat to end of round.

Round 3: Knit 8 (10, 12, 14), k2tog. Repeat to end of round.

Round 4: Knit 7 (9, 11, 13), k2tog. Repeat to end of round.

Round 5: Knit 6 (8, 10, 12), k2tog. Repeat to end of round.

Round 6: Knit 5 (7, 9, 11), k2tog. Repeat to end of round.

Round 7: Knit 4 (6, 8, 10), k2tog. Repeat to end of round.

Round 8: Knit 3 (5, 7, 9), k2tog. Repeat to end of round.

Round 9: Knit 2 (4, 6, 8), k2tog. Repeat to end of round.

Round 10: Knit 1 (3, 5, 7), k2tog. Repeat to end of round. For size 0–6 months, skip to round 17.

Round 11: Knit _ (2, 4, 6) k2tog. Repeat to end of round.

Round 12: Knit _ (1, 3, 5), k2tog. Repeat to end of round. For size 6–12 months, skip to round 17.

Round 13: Knit _ (_, 2, 4), k2tog. Repeat to end of round.

Round 14: Knit _ (_1, 3), k2tog. Repeat to end of round. For size 1–2 years, skip to round 17.

Round 15: Knit 2, k2tog.

Round 16: Knit 1, k2tog.

Round 17: K2tog. Repeat to end of round.

finishing

Make a very small pompom in B (see page 38) and attach to top of beret. Weave in all ends to finish.

The evenly spaced decreases in this pattern create a lovely pinwheel shape at the crown.

scarf hat

Why worry about keeping track of both a scarf and a hat? Combine the two and you've got this adorable hat-scarf, (or scarf-hat), for a wonderfully warm alternative to lugging around two pieces of clothing. Knit the scarf ends in thick stripes or keep it solid color, if you prefer.

SKILLS REQUIRED

Long-tail cast-on, knit 2 together (k2tog), joining new color, 3-needle bind-off, pompoms

YOU WILL NEED

- Size 9 (5.5mm) 12- or 16-inch circular needles and set of 4 or 5 double-pointed needles
- Blue Sky Alpacas Worsted Hand Dyes (50% alpaca, 50% merino; 3½ oz/100g/100 yards), 1 skein each in Chocolate 2016 (A) and Aqua 2017 (B). Also shown in Nectarine 2019 (A) and Strawberry 2018 (B), page 82.
- Stitch marker
- Yarn needle

GAUGE

16 stitches and 24 rounds = 4 inches in stockinette

SIZES

0–6 months (6–12 months, 1–2 years, 2 years and up)

FINISHED CIRCUMFERENCE

14 (16, 18, 20) inches

pattern

SCARF ENDS (make 2)

With A, cast on 10 (12, 12, 12) stitches.

Work in garter (knit every row) for 8 rows.

Switch to B.

Continue to work in garter stitch for 8 rows.

Switch to A.

Work in garter stitch, alternating colors as established, until entire scarf end measures 18 inches from cast-on edge. Leave stitches on needle; cut yarn and set aside.

HAT

With B, cast on 56 (64, 72, 80) stitches, place marker, and join to begin knitting in the round.

Round 1: Using 3-needle bind-off (see page 37), join across all stitches of first scarf end, knit 18 (20, 24, 28) stitches, join across stitches of second scarf end, knit 18 (20, 24, 28) stitches.

Work in garter stitch (knit one round, purl one round) for 8 rounds.

Change to stockinette (knit every round) until the hat measures 5 (5½, 6, 6½) inches from cast-on edge of brim.

baby beanies

DECREASING

Round 1: Knit 6, k2tog. Repeat to end of round.

Round 2 and all even-numbered rounds through round 10: Knit.

Round 3: Knit 5, k2tog. Repeat to end of round.

Round 5: Knit 4, k2tog. Repeat to end of round.

Round 7: Knit 3, k2tog. Repeat to end of round.

Round 9: Knit 2, k2tog. Repeat to end of round.

Round 11: Knit 1, k2tog. Repeat to end of round.

Round 12: K2tog. Repeat to end of round.

Cut yarn, leaving a 6-inch tail. Using a yarn needle, thread yarn through remaining stitches, and pull tightly to close hole. Weave in ends.

finishing

Using B, make 5 small pompoms (see page 38). Attach to ends of scarf and to top of hat as shown in photograph.

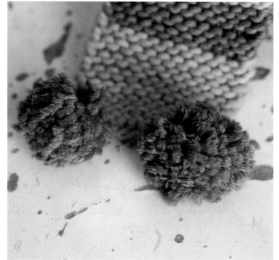

bedtime stocking cap

Ohhh, how I love this little cap! The two-tone ribbing is a modern touch but you could knit the band in one color only, if you prefer.

SKILLS REQUIRED
Long-tail cast on, joining new color,
knit 2 together (k2tog), tassels

YOU WILL NEED
- Size 9 (5.5mm) 12- or 16-inch circular
  needles and set of 4 or 5 double-pointed
  needles
- Jo Sharp Silkroad Aran (85% wool, 10% silk,
  5% cashmere; 1¾ oz/50g/93 yards),
  1 ball each of Bracken 454 (A),
  Cornsilk 107 (B), Ricepaper 108 (C),
  Venetian 101 (D), and Bud 457 (E)
- Stitch marker
- Yarn needle

GAUGE
16 stitches and 26 rounds = 4 inches

SIZES
0–6 months (6–12 months, 1–2 years,
2 years and up)

FINISHED CIRCUMFERENCE
14 (16, 18, 20) inches

pattern

With A, cast on 56 (64, 72, 80) stitches, place
marker, and join to begin knitting in the round.

Round 1: Knit 1 with A, purl 1 with B. Repeat to end
of round. Repeat this round 3 more times.

Knit in stripe pattern as follows: 6 rounds each of
C, D, B, E, A.

Work stripe pattern until hat measures 5 (5½, 6, 6 ½)
inches from cast-on edge.

DECREASING (keeping stripe pattern intact)
Round 1: Knit 6, k2tog. Repeat to end of round.

**Round 2 and all even-numbered rounds through
round 18:** Knit.

Round 3: Knit.

Round 5: Knit 5, k2tog

Round 7: Knit.

Round 9: Knit 4, k2tog. Repeat to end of round.

Rounds 11–19: Knit.

Round 20: Knit 3, k2tog. Repeat to end of round.

Rounds 21–30: Knit.

Round 31: Knit 2, k2tog. Repeat to end of round.

Rounds 32–41: Knit.

Round 42: Knit 1, k2tog. Repeat to end of round.

Rounds 43–48: Knit.

Continue to work in stockinette until last round of
current color repeat, then k2tog to end of round.

Cut yarn and, using a yarn needle, pull tail through
remaining stitches.

finishing

Make a tassel (see page 39) with A and attach to
top point of hat. Weave in all ends to finish.

garter and hearts

A simple hat made in a tweedy yarn makes a definite fashion statement. I have used garter stitch for this hat to bring out the best in the yarn, letting the natural texture and gorgeous colors make the statement. The felt heart shapes are sewn on afterward with a blanket stitch.

SKILLS REQUIRED

Long-tail cast-on, knit 2 together (k2tog), purl 2 together (p2tog), knit into front and back of stitch (kfb), 3-needle bind-off

YOU WILL NEED

- Size 9 (5.5mm) 12- or 16-inch circular needles and set of 4 or 5 double-pointed needles
- Colinette Prism (50% wool, 50% cotton; 3½ oz/100g/130 yards), 1 skein in either Frangipani 145 (shown opposite) or Toscana 55 (shown on page 89)
- Stitch marker
- Yarn needle
- One sheet of store-bought felt for heart appliqués
- Scrap yarn for sewing heart to hat

GAUGE

16 stitches and 32 rounds = 4 inches in garter stitch

SIZES

0–6 months (6–12 months, 1–2 years, 2 years and up)

FINISHED CIRCUMFERENCE

14 (16, 18, 20) inches

pattern

EARFLAPS (make 2)

With DPNs, cast on 3 stitches.

Row 1: Knit.

Row 2: Kfb, knit 1, kfb.

Row 3 and all odd-numbered rows through row 9: Knit.

Row 4: Kfb, knit 3, kfb.

Row 6: Kfb, knit 5, kfb.

Row 8: Kfb, knit 7, kfb.

Row 10: Kfb, knit 9, kfb (13 stitches).

Rows 11–13: Knit.

Cut yarn and set earflap aside.

HAT

Cast on 56 (64, 72, 80) stitches, place marker, and join to begin knitting in the round.

Round 1: Using 3-needle bind-off technique (see page 37), join across first earflap, knit 17 (21, 25, 29), join across second earflap, knit 17 (21, 25, 29).

Round 2: Purl.

Round 3: Knit.

Repeat rounds 2 and 3 until piece measures 5 (5½, 6, 6½) inches from cast-on edge, ending with a purl round.

DECREASING

Round 1: Knit 6, k2tog. Repeat to end of round.

Round 2 and all even-numbered rounds through round 10: Purl.

Round 3: Knit 5, k2tog. Repeat to end of round.

Round 5: Knit 4, k2tog. Repeat to end of round.

Round 7: Knit 3, k2tog. Repeat to end of round.

Round 9: Knit 2, k2tog. Repeat to end of round.

Round 11: Knit 1, k2tog. Repeat to end of round.

Round 12: P2tog. Repeat to end of round.

finishing

Weave in all ends. Cut two heart shapes from a piece of red felt using the template. Sew one heart on each side of the hat, just above the earflap, using a blanket stitch and a scrap of red yarn.

Cut out two hearts.

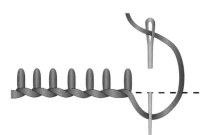

BLANKET STITCH

Working on the right side, put your needle in about ½ inch in from the edge of the heart and bring it out just outside the edge of the heart. Keeping the thread under the needle as shown, pull to tighten. Continue around the entire edge of the heart.

candy beret

The bright colors and little bobbles of this hat remind me of a bowl of candy, just begging to be gobbled up. The bobbles are made separately after the hat is finished and then sewn onto the hat. The Malabrigo wool yarn is as soft as butter and a dream to work with, and the slight color and texture variations of this hand-dyed yarn just add to the delight.

SKILLS REQUIRED

Long-tail cast-on, knit 2 together (k2tog), joining new color, make bobble (mb)

YOU WILL NEED

- Size 9 (5.5mm) 12- or 16-inch circular and set of 4 or 5 double-pointed needles
- Malabrigo Worsted Hand-Dyed Merino (100% merino wool; 3½ oz/100g/ 215 yards), 1 skein each in Apricot 72 (A), Pollen 19 (B), and Molly 39 (C)
- Stitch marker
- Yarn needle

GAUGE

16 stitches and 28 rounds = 4 inches

SIZES

0-6 months (6-12 months, 1-2 years, 2 years and up)

FINISHED CIRCUMFERENCE

12 (14, 16, 18) inches

TIP: With berets, I like a tighter fit at the brim since the hat is so large and floppy. If you prefer a looser fitting beret, simply knit the next size.

pattern

With A, cast on 48 (56, 64, 72) stitches, place marker, and join to begin knitting in the round.

Round 1: Knit 2, purl 2. Repeat to end of round.

Repeat round 1 seven more times.

Change to B.

Round 2: Knit.

Round 3: Knit 4, m1. Repeat to end of round.

Change to C.

Rounds 4-7: Knit.

Round 8: Knit 5, m1. Repeat to end of round.

Continue knitting in stockinette for 1 (1½, 2, 2½) inch(es).

Switch to A.

DECREASING

Round 1: Knit 10 (12, 14, 16), k2tog. Repeat to end of round.

Round 2: Knit 9 (11, 13, 15), k2tog. Repeat to end of round.

Round 3: Knit 8 (10, 12, 14), k2tog. Repeat to end of round.

Round 4: Knit 7 (9, 11, 13), k2tog. Repeat to end of round.

Round 5: Knit 6 (8, 10, 12), k2tog. Repeat to end of round.

Round 6: Knit 5 (7, 9, 11), k2tog. Repeat to end of round.

Round 7: Knit 4 (6, 8, 10), k2tog. Repeat to end of round.

Round 8: Knit 3 (5, 7, 9), k2tog. Repeat to end of round.

Round 9: Knit 2 (4, 6, 8), k2tog. Repeat to end of round.

Round 10: Knit 1 (3, 5, 7), k2tog. Repeat to end of round. For size 0–6 months, skip to round 15.

Round 11: Knit _ (2, 4, 6), k2tog. Repeat to end of round.

Round 12: Knit _ (1, 3, 5), k2tog. Repeat to end of round. For size 6–12 months, skip to round 15.

Round 13: Knit _ (_, 2, 4), k2tog. Repeat to end of round.

Round 14: Knit _ (_, 1, 3), k2tog. Repeat to end of round.

Round 15: K2tog. Repeat to end of round.

For size 2 years and up only, repeat round 15 one more time.

Cut yarn, leaving a 6-inch tail. Using a yarn needle, thread tail through remaining stitches and pull tightly to close.

finishing

With B, make 6 bobbles (see page 66).
Tie bobbles on to top of beret as shown in photograph. Weave in ends to finish.

stripes and pompoms

Let's face it, pompoms on baby clothes are darn cute. And babies can get away with wearing them without looking silly. The poms adorning the earflaps on this cap are larger than usual just for fun, and they look ridiculously cute framing a chubby baby face. The earflaps, too, are oversize to guarantee little heads and cheeks are kept warm and cozy in chilly weather.

pattern

EARFLAPS (make 2)

With A, cast on 3 stitches.

Row 1: Knit 1, m1, knit 1, m1, knit 1 (5 stitches).

Row 2 and all even-numbered rows through row 18: Purl.

Row 3: Knit 2, m1, knit 1, m1, knit 2.

Row 5: Knit 3, m1, knit 1, m1, knit 3.

Row 7: Knit 4, m1, knit 1, m1, knit 4.

Row 9: Knit 5, m1, knit 1, m1, knit 4.

Row 11: Knit 6, m1, knit 1, m1, knit 6.

Row 13: Knit 7, m1, knit 1, m1, knit 7 (17 stitches).

Skip to row 20 for 0–6 month size.

Row 15: Knit 8, m1, knit 1, m1, knit 8 (19 stitches).

Skip to row 20 for 6–12 month size.

Row 17: Knit 9, m1, knit 1, m1, knit 9 (21 stitches).

Skip to row 20 for 1–2 year size.

Row 19: Knit 10, m1, knit 1, m1, knit 10 (23 stitches).

Row 20: Purl.

Row 21: Knit.

Cut yarn, leaving a 20-inch tail. Leave earflaps on needle.

HAT

Round 1: This round is a little tricky, but the result is worth it! Knit across all 17 (19, 21, 23) stitches of first earflap using circular needle, weaving the yarn tail in behind as you go. With the yarn tail and working yarn, use the long-tail cast-on method to cast on another 11 (13, 15, 17) stitches. Knit across second earflap, again weaving in the yarn tail behind the work as you go. Cast on another 11 (13, 15, 17) stitches. Place marker and join to begin knitting in the round.

Round 2: Purl 1, knit 1 for 11 (13, 15, 17) stitches, knit 17 (19, 21, 23), purl 1, knit 1 for 11 (13, 15, 17) stitches, knit 17 (19, 21, 23).

Round 3: Knit 1, purl 1 for 11 (13, 15, 17) stitches, knit 17 (19, 21, 23), knit 1, purl 1 for 11 (13, 15, 17) stitches, knit 17 (19, 21, 23) stitches.

Round 4: Repeat round 2.

Round 5: Repeat round 3.

Round 6: Knit.

stripe pattern

Alternate between knitting 6 rounds of B and 6 rounds of A.

Following stripe pattern, continue working in stockinette until piece measures 5 (5½, 6, 6½) inches from cast-on edge of brim.

DECREASING

Continue to knit in established stripe pattern as you decrease.

Round 1: Knit 6, k2tog. Repeat to end of round.

Round 2 and all even-numbered rounds through round 10: Knit.

Round 3: Knit 5, k2tog. Repeat to end of round.

Round 5: Knit 4, k2tog. Repeat to end of round.

Round 7: Knit 3, k2tog. Repeat to end of round.

Round 9: Knit 2, k2tog. Repeat to end of round.

Round 11: Knit 1, k2tog. Repeat to end of round.

Round 12: K2tog. Repeat to end of round.

Cut yarn, leaving a 6-inch tail, and using a yarn needle thread through remaining stitches. Pass through hole at center of the hat and pull tightly to close.

finishing

With B, create two 2½-inch pompoms (see page 38) and attach one to the bottom of each earflap, trimming as necessary. Weave in all ends to finish.

SEED STITCH

Seed Stitch is a pattern made by alternating a row of knit 1, purl 1 with a row of purl 1, knit 1. The result is a knitted fabric that is bumpy and looks the same on both sides. It lies flat, making it a great stitch to use for the band on this hat and on the Cabled Greens hat on page 136.

frilly hat

I was inspired to create this hat after watching my girls playing in their little tutus, observing the way the ruffles swirled out and bounced around. The frilled edge on this hat is very easy, although slightly more time-consuming to make than a normal brim. Worked in a light purple shade with a darker slate trim, it isn't over-the-top girly.

SKILLS REQUIRED
Long-tail cast on, knit 3 together (k3tog), knit 2 together (k2tog), joining new color, pompoms

YOU WILL NEED
- Size 7 (4.5mm) 12- or 16-inch circular needles and set of 4 or 5 double-pointed needles
- Knit Picks Wool of the Andes (100% Peruvian Highland wool; 1¾ oz/50g/110 yards) 1 skein each in Iris Heather 24070 (A) and Mist 23538 (B).
- Stitch marker
- Yarn needle
- 1¼-inch button (optional; skip for younger babies)

GAUGE
20 stitches and 26 rounds = 4 inches in stockinette

SIZES
0–6 months (6–12 months, 1–2 years, 2 years and up)

FINISHED CIRCUMFERENCE
11¼ (12¾, 14½, 16) inches

pattern

With A, cast on 168 (192, 216, 240) stitches, place marker, and join to begin knitting in the round.

Round 1: Knit all stitches.

Round 2: Purl all stitches.

Round 3: Purl all stitches.

Round 4: Knit all stitches.

Round 5: Purl all stitches.

Round 6: K3tog. Repeat until end of round— 56, (64, 72, 80) stitches.

Change to B.

Round 1: Knit 1, purl 1. Repeat until end of round.

Continue to work in knit 1, purl 1 ribbing for 8 more rounds.

Change to A.

Round 1: Knit all stitches.

Continue to work in stockinette stitch until piece measures 5 (5½, 6, 6½) inches from the start of ribbing.

baby beanies

DECREASING

Round 1: Knit 6, k2tog. Repeat to end of round.

Round 2 and all even-numbered rounds through round 10: Knit.

Round 3: Knit 5, k2tog. Repeat to end of round.

Round 5: Knit 4, k2tog. Repeat to end of round.

Round 7: Knit 3, k2tog. Repeat to end of round.

Round 9: Knit 2, k2tog. Repeat to end of round.

Round 11: Knit 1, k2tog. Repeat to end of round.

Round 12: K2tog. Repeat to end of round.

Cut yarn, leaving a 6-inch tail. Using yarn needle, thread tail through remaining stitches and pull tightly to close hole and secure.

finishing

With B, make a 2-inch pompom (see page 38) and attach it to the top of the hat. If you like, with A, sew a large button onto the ribbing section of the hat. (For safety reasons, it's best to leave the button off for younger babies.).

soft as a cloud

Delicate and indulgent in a deliciously touchable angora-blend yarn, this hat really is as soft and fluffy as a cloud. Knit it as a luxurious gift for a new mother, or make one to spoil your own little cherub.

SKILLS REQUIRED
Long-tail cast-on, knit 2 together (k2tog), i-cord

YOU WILL NEED
- Size 7 (4.5mm) 12- or 16-inch circular needles and set of 4 or 5 double-pointed needles
- Filatura Di Crosa Zara (100% merino extrafine wool, 1¾ oz/50 g/136 yards), 1 ball in Rose 1022 (A)
- Anny Blatt Angora Super (70% angora, 30% wool; 1 oz/25g/116 yards), 1 skein in Braise 876 (B)
- Stitch marker
- Yarn needle

GAUGE
20 stitches and 32 rounds = 4 inches with B in stockinette

SIZES
0–6 months (6–12 months, 1–2 years, 2 years and up)

FINISHED CIRCUMFERENCE
12¾ (14½, 16, 17½) inches

pattern

With A, cast on 64 (72, 80, 88) stitches, place marker, and join to begin knitting in the round.

Round 1: Knit.

Round 2: Purl.

Repeat rounds 1 and 2 six more times.

Change to B.

Round 1: Knit.

Continue working in stockinette until piece measures 5 (5½, 6, 6½) inches from cast-on edge.

DECREASING
Round 1: Knit 6, k2tog. Repeat to end of round.

Round 2 and all even-numbered rounds through round 10: Knit.

Round 3: Knit 5, k2tog. Repeat to end of round.

Round 5: Knit 4, k2tog. Repeat to end of round.

Round 7: Knit 3, k2tog. Repeat to end of round.

Round 9: Knit 2, k2tog. Repeat to end of round.

Round 11: Knit 1, k2tog. Repeat to end of round.

Round 12: K2tog. Repeat to end of round.

Cut yarn, leaving a 6-inch tail. Using a yarn needle, thread tail through remaining stitches and pull tightly to close hole and secure.

baby beanies

finishing

With A and a DPN, cast on 4 stitches and work 20 inches of i-cord (see page 38). Bind off and sew beginning and end of i-cord together. Fold i-cord in half twice. Tie a piece of scrap yarn tightly around center of loops, then attach to top of the hat. Weave in all ends to finish.

chocqua

I don't know about you, but I adore chocolate brown and aqua blue together. The combination looks equally lovely on boys and girls, especially as a nice alternative to typical "girl" and "boy" shades. The stranded pattern here is extremely simple, making it perfect for a first-time Fair Isle project. See page 69 for more on Fair Isle knitting.

SKILLS REQUIRED
Long-tail cast-on, knit 2 together (k2tog), joining new color, 3-needle bind-off, tassels

YOU WILL NEED
- Size 7 (4.5mm) 12- or 16-inch straight or circular needles and set of 4 or 5 double-pointed needles
- Cascade 220 Wool (100% Peruvian Highland wool; 3½ oz/100g/220 yards), 1 skein each Cordovan 9408 (A) and Summer Sky 7815 (B)
- Stitch marker
- Yarn needle

GAUGE
20 stitches and 28 rounds = 4 inches

SIZES
0–6 months (6–12 months, 1–2 years, 2 years and up)

FINISHED CIRCUMFERENCE
12¾ (14½, 16, 17½) inches

pattern

With A, cast on 64 (72, 80, 88) stitches, place marker, and join to begin knitting in the round.

Round 1: Knit 1, purl 1. Continue to end of round.

Round 2: Purl 1, knit 1. Continue to end of round.

Repeat rounds 1 and 2 four more times. Change to B.

TIP: When knitting with two colors at once, wrap the yarn around a spare finger of your right hand. It takes some practice, but you can knit with your index and middle fingers alternating between colors. Remember to keep your stitches loose when stranding to avoid puckers.

Round 1: Knit.

Round 2: With B, knit 3. With A, knit 1. Repeat to end of round.

Round 3: With B, knit all stitches.

Round 4: With A, knit 1. With B, knit 3. Repeat to end of round.

Round 5: With B, knit all stitches.

Round 6: With B, knit 3. With A, knit 1. Repeat to end of round.

Round 7: With B, knit all stitches.

Round 8: With A, knit all stitches.

Round 9: With B, knit 1. With A, knit 3. Repeat to end of round.

Round 10: With A, knit all stitches.

Round 11: With A, knit 3. With B, knit 1. Repeat to end of round.

Round 12: With A, knit all stitches.

Round 13: With B, knit 1. With A, knit 3. Repeat to end of round.

Round 14: With A, knit all stitches.

Repeat rounds 1–14 for pattern. Continue in pattern until piece measures 6 (6½, 7, 7½) inches from the cast-on edge, ending with last round of pattern sequence.

Bind off all stitches using 3-needle bind-off technique (see page 37).

finishing

With combination of A and B, make two 4-inch tassels (see page 39) and attach to top corner points of the hat. Weave in all ends.

VARIATIONS ON A THEME

You can take this same basic hat shape and mix in your own colors and patterns to create exactly the hat you want. Here are two totally different looks—one with stripes (above) and one in bold solids (opposite)—and both equally cute.

sweet spring

Soft dandelion green, light airy blue, and a little splash of pink make for a deliciously springtime hat. Knit in a cotton and microfiber blend, it's light and cool enough for April days. Add just one flower as I have here, or make a whole bunch and create a little garden on your hat.

SKILLS REQUIRED

Long-tail cast-on, knit 2 together (k2tog), joining new color, i-cord

YOU WILL NEED

- Size 9 (5.5mm) 12- or 16-inch circular needle and set of 4 or 5 double-pointed needles
- Jo Sharp Desert Garden Aran (65% cotton 35% microfiber; 1¾ oz/50g/ 60 yards), 1 ball each of Dandelion 238 (A) and Boat 660 (B) and small amount of Arizona 666 (C) for flower
- Stitch marker
- Yarn needle
- Embroidery thread to match yarn C
- ¾-inch button (optional; skip for younger babies)

GAUGE

16 stitches and 24 rounds = 4 inches

SIZES

0–6 months (6–12 months, 1–2 years, 2 years and up)

FINISHED CIRCUMFERENCE

14 (16, 18, 20) inches

pattern

With A, cast on 56 (64, 72, 80) stitches, place marker, and join to begin knitting in the round. Work in stockinette (knit every round) until piece measures 1½ (2, 2, 2½) inches from cast-on edge.

Change to B.

Continue to work in stockinette until piece measures 5 (5½, 6, 6½) inches from cast-on edge.

DECREASING

Round 1: Knit 6, k2tog. Repeat to end of round.

Round 2 and all even-numbered round through round 10: Knit.

Round 3: Knit 5, k2tog. Repeat to end of round.

Round 5: Knit 4, k2tog. Repeat to end of round.

Round 7: Knit 3, k2tog. Repeat to end of round.

Round 9: Knit 2, k2tog. Repeat to end of round.

Round 11: Knit 1, k2tog. Repeat to end of round.

Round 12: K2tog. Repeat to end of round.

Cut yarn, leaving a 6-inch tail. Using a yarn needle, thread tail through remaining stitches and pull tightly to close hole and secure.

FLOWER

With C and circular (or double-pointed) needle, cast on 55 stitches.

Row 1: Knit.

Row 2: Knit 1, bind off 9. *Knit 2, bind off 9*. Repeat from * to * until end of row.

Cut yarn, leaving a 6-inch tail. Using a yarn needle, thread tail through remaining loops and pull tightly to close circle. Weave in ends.

finishing

Using embroidery thread, sew flower to hat. If you like, sew a button on top of flower center. (For safety reasons, it's best to leave the button off for younger babies.) Weave in all ends to finish.

snow bunny

Designed with the baby daughter of a friend of mine in mind, I chose a super-soft and fuzzy angora blend yarn for this hat, which is reminiscent to me of snow, in pastel pink and green to suit her coloring. See another version of the hat in blue and green on page 116.

SKILLS REQUIRED

Long-tail cast-on, knit 2 together (k2tog), joining new color, 3-needle bind-off, tassels

YOU WILL NEED

- Size 9 (5.5mm) 12- or 16-inch straight or circular needles and set of 4 or 5 double-pointed needles
- Naturally Sensation (70% merino, 30% angora; 1¾ oz/50g/131 yards), 1 skein each in Pink 307 (A), White 300 (B), and Green 302 (C)
- Stitch marker
- Yarn needle

GAUGE

16 stitches and 28 rounds = 4 inches

SIZES

0-6 months (6-12 months, 1-2 years, 2 years and up)

FINISHED CIRCUMFERENCE

14 (16, 18, 20) inches

pattern

EARFLAPS (make 2)

With A, cast on 3 stitches.

Row 1 and all odd-numbered rows through row 7: Knit.

Row 2: Kfb, knit 1, kfb.

Row 4: Kfb, knit 3, kfb.

Row 6: Kfb, knit 5, kfb.

Row 8: Kfb, knit 7, kfb.

Rows 9-13: Knit.

Cut yarn and set aside.

HAT

Cast on 56 (64, 72, 80) stitches, place marker, and join to begin knitting in the round.

Round 1: Knit 17 (21, 25, 29) stitches. Using the 3-needle bind-off technique, join across 11 stitches of earflap, knit 17 (21, 25, 29) stitches, join across 11 stitches of second earflap.

Round 2: Purl.

Round 3: Knit.

Round 4: Purl.

Round 5: Knit.

Round 6: Purl.

Change to B.

Round 1: Knit.

Continue in stockinette for 5 (8, 10, 12) more rounds.

Change to C.

Round 1: Purl.

Round 2: Knit.

Round 3: Knit.

Round 4: Knit.

Change to A.

Round 1: Purl.

Round 2: Knit.

Continue in stockinette for 5 (8, 10, 12) more rounds.

Change to B.

Round 1: Purl.

Continue in stockinette (knit every round) until piece measures 5 (5½, 6, 6½) inches from cast-on edge.

DECREASING

Round 1: Knit 6, k2tog. Repeat to end of round.

Round 2 and all even-numbered rounds through round 10: Knit.

Round 3: Knit 5, k2tog. Repeat to end of round.

Round 5: Knit 4, k2tog. Repeat to end of round.

Round 7: Knit 3, k2tog. Repeat to end of round.

Round 9: Knit 2, k2tog. Repeat to end of round.

Round 11: Knit 1, k2tog. Repeat to end of round.

Round 12: K2tog. Repeat to end of round.

Cut yarn, leaving a 6-inch tail. Using a yarn needle, thread tail through remaining stitches and pull tightly to close hole and secure.

finishing

Make the tassels (see page 39) using several 20 to 24-inch lengths of B and C. Fold a bunch in half and gently ease them through the stitches at the bottom of one earflap for about 1 inch. Make a slipknot with yarn tails and tighten. Make a second tassel for the other side. Braid the tassels if you prefer.

pixie hood

I just love this little hood! It frames the face much like a traditional bonnet, but the little pointed top and long braided ties give it a bit of quirky charm.

SKILLS REQUIRED
Long-tail cast-on, knit 2 together (k2tog), pick up and knit, slip 1 stitch (sl1), pass slipped stitch over (psso), tassels

YOU WILL NEED
- Size 9 (5.5mm) straight needle and set of 4 or 5 double-pointed needles
- Malabrigo Worsted Hand-Dyed Merino (100% merino wool; 3½ oz/100g/215 yards), 1 skein each in Pigeon 507 (A) and Rattan 504 (B)
- Yarn needle

GAUGE
16 stitches and 28 rows = 4 inches

SIZES
0–6 months (6-12 months, 1–2 years, 2 years and up)

pattern

With A and straight needles, cast on 48 (56, 64, 72) stitches.

Row 1: Knit 1, purl 1. Repeat to end of row.

Row 2: Purl 1, knit 1. Repeat to end of row.

Row 3: Knit 1, purl 1. Repeat to end of row.

Row 4: Purl 1, knit 1. Repeat to end of row.

Change to B.

Row 5: Knit.

Row 6: Purl.

Continue to work in stockinette, repeating rows 5 and 6 for 1 (1, 1½, 1½) more inches.

BEGIN SHAPING
Row 1: Slip 1, knit 1, psso, knit to last 2 stitches, k2tog.

Row 2: Purl.

Row 3: Knit.

Row 4: Purl.

Repeat rows 1–4 two more times.

Continue knitting in stockinette until piece measures 4½ (5½, 6½, 7½) inches from the cast-on edge. Divide stitches evenly between two DPNs. Turn work inside out and cast off remaining stitches together using 3-needle bind-off method.

With A, pick up and knit 1 stitch every 2 stitches along the front edge.

Row 1: Knit 1, purl 1. Repeat to end of row.

Row 2: Purl 1, knit 1. Repeat to end of row.

Row 3: Knit 1, purl 1. Repeat to end of row.

Row 4: Purl 1, knit 1. Repeat to end of row.

Bind off all stitches following rib pattern.

finishing

With B, make two small tassels. Cut six 16-inch lengths of A. Loop 3 strands of A through the top loops of each tassel. Braid these strands together and then attach each tie to inside front corner of the hat. Weave in ends to finish.

circus stripes

Whimsical stripes and a little i-cord knot at the top of this hat make it a joy to wear and even nicer to look at. The organic cotton yarn is wonderfully soft to work with.

SKILLS REQUIRED
Long-tail cast-on, joining new color, knit 2 together (k2tog), i-cord

YOU WILL NEED
- Size 9 (5.5mm) 12- or 16-inch circular and set of 4 or 5 double-pointed needles
- Blue Sky Alpacas Dyed Cotton (100% organically grown cotton; 3½ oz/100g/ 150 yards), 1 skein each in Shrimp 609 (A) and Circus Peanut 631 (B)
- Stitch marker
- Yarn needle

GAUGE
16 stitches and 28 rounds = 4 inches

SIZES
0–6 months (6–12 months, 1–2 years, 2 years and up)

FINISHED CIRCUMFERENCE
14 (16, 18, 20) inches

pattern

With A, cast on 56 (64, 72, 80) stitches, place marker, and join to begin knitting in the round.

Round 1: Knit.

Round 2: Purl.

Repeat rounds 1 and 2 four more times.

Work in stockinette stitch (knit every round) for 1 inch.

Change to B.

Round 1: Knit.

Round 2: Purl.

Change to A.

Knit 5 rounds of stockinette.

Repeat the above 7 rounds in pattern (purl 2 rounds in B; knit 5 rounds in A) until piece measures 5 (5½, 6, 6½) inches from cast-on edge.

DECREASING
Continue in pattern as established, purling rounds 6 and 7 with A and incorporating decreases as indicated.
Note: If decreases fall on round 6 or 7, substitute purl and p2tog for knit and k2tog.

Round 1: Knit 6, k2tog. Repeat to end of round.

Round 2: Knit.

Round 3: Knit 5, k2tog. Repeat to end of round.

Round 4: Knit.

Round 5: Knit 4, k2tog. Repeat to end of round.

Rounds 6–9: Knit.

Round 10: Knit 3, k2tog. Repeat to end of round.

Rounds 11–16: Knit.

Round 17: Knit 2, k2tog. Repeat to end of round.

Rounds 18–25: Knit.

Round 26: Knit 1, k2tog. Repeat to end of round.

Continue in A only to end of hat.

Rounds 27–31: Knit.

Round 32: K2tog. Repeat to end of round.

Continue to k2tog until only 4 stitches remain. Work i-cord (see page 38) for 6 inches, then bind off all stitches.

finishing

Knot i-cord at top of the hat. Using a yarn needle, thread tail through middle of i-cord and down into hat, pulling end of i-cord just under the first loop of the knot. Weave in all ends to finish.

little boy blue

This young fellow has the same gorgeous blue eyes as my oldest son, the kind of eyes I always dreamed of having. The eyes have a darker band around the edge that makes them really stand out and I was inspired to use these two shades of blue in a whimsical hat.

Rounds 5–6: Purl.

Change to A.

Rounds 7–10: Knit.

Change to B.

Continue working in stockinette until piece measures 5 (5½, 6, 6½) inches from cast-on edge.

DECREASING

Round 1: Knit 6, k2tog. Repeat to end of round.

Round 2: Knit.

Round 3: Knit 5, k2tog. Repeat to end of round.

Round 4: Knit.

Change to C.

Rounds 5–6: Purl.

Change to A.

Round 7: Knit 4, k2tog. Repeat to end of round.

Round 8: Knit.

Round 9: Knit 3, k2tog. Repeat to end of round.

Round 10: Knit.

Change to B.

Rounds 11–16: Knit.

Round 17: Knit 2, k2tog. Repeat to end of round.

Rounds 18–22: Knit.

Round 23: Knit 1, k2tog. Repeat to end of round.

Rounds 24–26: Knit.

Round 27: K2tog. Repeat to end of round.

Cut yarn, leaving a 6-inch tail. Using a yarn needle, thread through remaining stitches and pull tightly to close.

finishing

With C, make a tassel (see page 39) and attach to top point of hat. Weave in all ends to finish.

SKILLS REQUIRED

Long-tail cast-on, knit 2 together (k2tog), joining new color, tassels

YOU WILL NEED

- Size 9 (5.5mm) 12- or 16-inch circular needles and set of 4 or 5 double-pointed needles
- Jo Sharp Silkroad Aran (85% wool, 10% silk, 5% cashmere; 1¾ oz/50g/93 yards), 1 ball each of Stone 452 (A), Empire 137 (B), and Parchment 112 (C)
- Stitch marker
- Yarn needle

GAUGE

16 stitches and 26 rounds = 4 inches in stockinette

SIZES

0–6 months (6–12 months, 1–2 years, 2 years and up)

FINISHED CIRCUMFERENCE

14 (16, 18, 20) inches

pattern

Using A, cast on 56 (64, 72, 80) stitches, place marker, and join to begin knitting in the round.

Round 1: Knit 1, purl 1. Repeat to end of round.

Round 2: Purl 1, knit 1. Repeat to end of round.

Round 3: Knit 1, purl 1. Repeat to end of round.

Round 4: Purl 1, knit 1. Repeat to end of round.

Change to B.

Work in stockinette (knit every round) for 1½ (2, 2, 2½) inch(es) more.

Change to C.

classic cap

This hat is easier to make than it looks at first glance. Simple knit and purl stitches form the raised brocade-type pattern and a slightly more intricate, but still very easy, series of slipped stitches give the brim texture. A braided cord and chunky tassel finish the look.

SKILLS REQUIRED

Long-tail cast-on, knit 2 together (k2tog), Slip 1 knitwise (s1kw), Slip 1 purlwise (s1pw), tassels

YOU WILL NEED

• Size 9 (5.5mm) 12- or 16-inch circular or straight needles and set of 4 or 5 double-pointed needles
• Malabrigo Worsted Hand-Dyed Merino (100% merino wool, 3½ oz/100g/ 215 yards), 1 skein in Cognac 158
• Stitch marker
• Yarn needle

GAUGE

16 stitches and 28 rounds = 4 inches

SIZES

0–6 months (6–12 months, 1–2 years, 2 years and up)

FINISHED CIRCUMFERENCE

14 (16, 18, 20) inches

pattern

Cast on 56, (64, 72, 80) stitches, place marker, and join to begin knitting in the round.

Round 1: Knit all stitches.

Round 2: Purl all stitches.

Round 3: Slip 1 stitch purlwise (s1pw), knit 1. Repeat to end of round.

Round 4: Purl 1, * with yarn in back (wyib) slip 1 stitch knitwise (s1kw), with yarn in front (wyif) purl 1 stitch*. Repeat from * to * until end of round.

Round 5: Knit all stitches.

Round 6: Purl all stitches.

Round 7: S1pw, wyib, knit 1. Repeat to end of round.

Round 8: Wyib, s1kw, wyib, purl 1. Repeat to end of round.

Round 9: Knit all stitches.

Round 10: Purl all stitches.

TIP: For a wider brim, repeat the above 10 rounds once or twice more.

Continue to work in stockinette stitch for ½, (1, 1½, 1½) inches.

Round 1: Purl 1, knit 7. Repeat to end of round.

Round 2: Purl 1, knit 1, purl 1, knit 5. Repeat to end of round.

Round 3: Purl 1, knit 3. Repeat to end of round.

Round 4: Purl 1, knit 5, purl 1, knit 1. Repeat to end of round.

Round 5: Purl 1, knit 7. Repeat to end of round.

Round 6: Repeat round 4.

Round 7: Repeat round 3.

Round 8: Repeat round 2.

Repeat rounds 1–8 once more.

Round 9: Purl 1, knit 7. Repeat to end of round.

Rounds 10–12: Knit all stitches.

DECREASING

Round 1: Knit 6 stitches, k2tog. Repeat to end of round.

Rounds 2, 4, 6: Knit all stitches.

Round 3: Knit 5, k2tog. Repeat to end of round.

Round 5: Knit 4, k2tog. Repeat to end of round.

Round 7: Knit 3, k2tog. Repeat to end of round.

Round 8: Knit 2, k2tog. Repeat to end of round.

Round 9: Knit all stitches.

Round 10: Knit 1, k2tog. Repeat to end of round.

Round 11: K2tog. Repeat to end of round.

Cut yarn, leaving 6-inch tail. Using a yarn needle, thread tail through remaining stitches and pull tightly to close circle and secure.

finishing

Cut 6 lengths of yarn twice the length of desired braid. Knot all threads together at one end and braid the lengths together. Make a 3-inch-long tassel (see page 39) and attach to braid. Attach braid and tassel to top of hat and weave in all ends to finish.

teddy hood

What could be cuter than a kid in a hood? Teddy bear ears on that hood, of course! Here I've combined pale gray and a deep burgundy for a stunning and slightly unusual color combination, and I used a nubby cotton yarn for extra texture that helps bring out that "teddy bear" look.

SKILLS REQUIRED
Long-tail cast-on, joining new color, pick up and knit

YOU WILL NEED
- Size 7 (4.5mm) 16-inch circular or straight needles
- Mission Falls 1824 Cotton (100% cotton; 1¾ oz/50g/85 yards), 1 skein each of Fog 400 (A) and Merlot 208 (B)
- Stitch marker
- Yarn needle

GAUGE
16 stitches and 28 rows = 4 inches

SIZES
0–6 months (6–12 months, 1–2 years, 2 years and up)

Finished measurement from chin around top of head to chin (excluding ties): 13 (15, 17, 19) inches

pattern

With A, cast on 48 (56, 64, 72) stitches.

Row 1: Knit 1, purl 1. Repeat to end of row.

Row 2: Knit 1, purl 1. Repeat to end of row.

Repeat rows 1 and 2 one more time.

Change to B.

Work in stockinette (knit one row, purl one row) until piece measures 4 (4½, 5, 5½) inches from cast-on edge.

Next row: Bind off 16 (19, 22, 25), knit 16 (18, 20, 22), bind off remaining 16 (19, 22, 25).

Row 1: With wrong side of work facing, reattach yarn and purl all stitches.

Row 2: Knit.

Continue to work in stockinette stitch until back "flap" when folded over measures ½ inch less than the length of front piece. Bind off remaining stitches. The result is a T-shaped piece of knitting. Fold the hat into bonnet shape and seam.

With A, and right side of work facing, pick up and knit every second stitch along bottom sides of hood, pick up every stitch along back of bottom of hood, and then pick up every second stitch along remaining side of hood, ensuring an even number of stitches.

baby beanies

Row 1: Knit 1, purl 1. Repeat to end of row.

Row 2: Purl 1, knit 1. Repeat to end of row.

Repeat rows 1 and 2 one more time and bind off all stitches.

EARS (make 2)
With A, cast on 11 stitches.

Row 1: Knit 1, purl 1. Repeat to end of row.

Repeat row 1 three more times.

Continue in moss stitch pattern (knit 1, purl 1), decreasing by k2tog at beginning and end of every second row until 3 stitches remain. Bind off stitches and cut yarn.

finishing

Fold ears in half and sew to top of hood using the photograph as reference. Make 2 small tassels (see page 39) and 2 braided cords, each with 6 strands of A. Attach to front bottom corners of hood. Weave in all ends to finish.

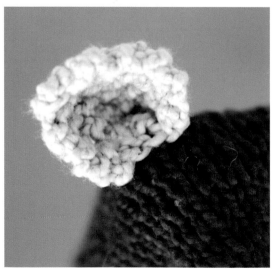

SEAMING

To seam a hat that is T-shaped, you will use a horizontal-to-vertical seam because you are joining one section of the hat where the knitted stitches are horizontal to another section where the stitches are vertical. This is not nearly as complicated as it sounds!

With a tapestry needle threaded with the same yarn you used to knit the hat, pick up one stitch from the horizontal section and then one stitch from the vertical knitting, making sure to go under both parts of the stitch, as shown. Pull on the yarn just until the two knitted sections meet. Do not pull so tightly that the seam puckers.

cabled greens

Cables can seem a little scary at first, but they really are simple. I mean, seriously, if I can cable, you can, too! This hat features one large winding cable up the center panel, and it is far easier to create than it looks. If you've never tried cabling before, give this a go and discover just how addictive it can be.

SKILLS REQUIRED
Long-tail cast-on, joining new color, knit 2 together (k2tog), cabling, tassels

YOU WILL NEED
- Size 9 (5.5mm) 12- or 16-inch circular needles and set of 4 or 5 double-pointed needles
- Mission Falls 1824 Wool (Merino super-wash wool; 1¾ oz/50g/85 yards), 1 ball each in Sprout 531 (A) and Basil 532 (B)
- Stitch marker
- Cable needle
- Yarn needle

GAUGE
16 stitches and 24 rounds = 4 inches

SIZES
0–6 months (6–12 months, 1–2 years, 2 years and up)

FINISHED CIRCUMFERENCE
14 (16, 18, 20) inches

Cable pattern: C8 = Slip next 4 stitches onto cable needle and hold in back of work, knit next 4 stitches from left-hand needle, and then knit 4 stitches from cable needle.

pattern

With A, cast on 56 (64, 72, 80) stitches, place marker, and join to begin knitting in the round.

Round 1: Knit 1, purl 1. Repeat to end of round.

Round 2: Purl 1, knit 1. Repeat to end of round.

Repeat rounds 1 and 2 one more time. Change to B.

Round 3: Knit 19 (23, 27, 31), purl 5, knit 8, purl 5, knit 19 (23, 27, 31).

Repeat round 3 more times.

Round 4: Knit 19 (23, 27, 31), purl 5, C8, purl 5, knit 19 (23, 27, 31).

Rounds 5–9: Repeat round 3.

Round 10: Knit 19 (23, 27, 31), purl 5, C8, purl 5, knit 19 (23, 27, 31).

baby beanies

Rounds 11–15: Repeat round 3.

Stop here for 0–6 months; other sizes continue.

Round 16: Knit 19 (23, 27, 31), purl 5, C8, purl 5, knit 19 (23, 27, 31).

Rounds 17–18: Repeat round 3. Stop here for sizes 6–12 months and 1–2 years.

Rounds 19–21: Repeat round 3.

DECREASING (all sizes)
Round 1: Knit 6, k2tog. Repeat to end of round.

Rounds 2, 4, 6: Knit.

Round 3: Knit 5, k2tog. Repeat to end of round.

Round 5: Knit 4, k2tog. Repeat to end of round.

Round 7: Knit 3, k2tog. Repeat to end of round.

Round 8: Knit 2, k2tog. Repeat to end of round.

Round 9: Knit.

Round 10: Knit 1, k2tog. Repeat to end of round.

Round 11: K2tog. Repeat to end of round.

Cut yarn, leaving a 6-inch tail. Using a yarn needle, thread tail through remaining stitches and pull tightly to close circle and secure.

finishing

With A, make a very full tassel (see page 39) and attach to top point of hat. Weave in all ends to finish.

MAKING CABLES

A cable is a winding rope in the knitted
fabric that is created by knitting the
stitches out of order.

1. Slip a number of stitches (the pattern you
   are knitting will tell you how many; in these
   illustrations it's 3) onto a cable needle or a
   double-pointed needle.

2. Bring these stitches in front of the work, as
   shown here, or behind the work (again, the
   pattern will tell you which way), and knit
   the next number of stitches (here it's 3) on
   the left needle.

3. Knit the 3 stitches on the cable needle or
   DPN.

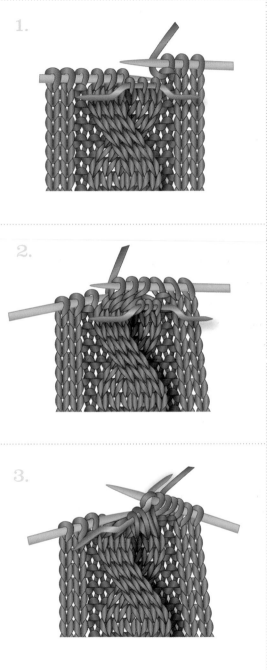

1.

2.

3.

color pop! beanie

Craving a little color in the middle of winter? This hat is just the thing to brighten up your day! Bright pink and green make a bold color statement, with a cream and pink flower for sweet decoration.

pattern

With A, cast on 64 (72, 80, 88) stitches, place marker, and join to begin knitting in the round.

Round 1: Knit 2, purl 2.

Repeat round 1 seven more times.

Change to B.

Round 2: Knit.

Round 3: Knit 1, purl 1. Repeat to end of round.

Round 4: Purl 1, knit 1. Repeat to end of round.

Repeat rounds 3 and 4 four more times.

Round 5: Knit.

Change to A.

Continue to work in stockinette stitch (knit every round) until piece measures 5 (5½, 6, 6½) inches from cast-on edge.

DECREASING
Round 1: Knit 6, k2tog. Repeat to end of round.

Rounds 2, 4, 6: Knit.

Round 3: Knit 5, k2tog. Repeat to end of round.

Round 5: Knit 4, k2tog. Repeat to end of round.

Round 7: Knit 3, k2tog. Repeat to end of round.

Round 8: Knit 2, k2tog. Repeat to end of round.

Round 9: Knit.

Round 10: Knit 1, k2tog. Repeat to end of round.

baby beanies

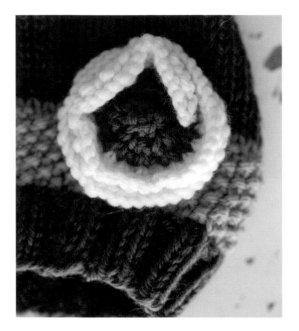

Round 11: K2tog. Repeat to end of round.

Cut yarn, leaving a 6-inch tail. Using a yarn needle, thread tail through remaining stitches and pull tightly to close circle and secure.

MAKE FLOWER

With DPNs and A, cast on 12 stitches.

Row 1: Kfb to end of row (24 stitches).

Row 2: Purl.

Row 3: Kfb to end of row (48 stitches).

Change to C.

Row 4: Purl.

Row 5: Kfb to end of row (96 stitches).

Row 6: Purl.

Row 7: Bind off all stitches.

Cut yarn, leaving a 12-inch tail.

finishing

Curl the flower around on itself to form a flower shape. Using the yarn needle and remaining tail, sew in place, using photograph as reference. Weave in all ends to finish.

resources

Need help finding the gorgeous yarns used in this book? Here are the yarn company websites. Then, with yarn in hand, check out these helpful knitting websites and forums!

YARN MANUFACTURERS

Anny Blatt: www.annyblatt.com
Blue Sky Alpacas: www.blueskyalpacas.com
Brown Sheep: www.brownsheep.com
Cascade Yarns: www.cascadeyarns.com
Colinette Yarns: www.colinette.com
Filatura Di Crosa: www.tahkistacycharles.com
Jo Sharp: www.josharp.com.au
KnitPicks: www.knitpicks.com
Malabrigo: www.malabrigoyarn.com
Mission Falls: www.missionfalls.com
Naturally Yarns: www.naturallyyarnsnz.com

HELPFUL WEBSITES

Ravelry: www.ravelry.com
THE place to go for knitters. Basically, everything you could ever want in a knitting website, all bundled up in one pretty package. Share your yarn "stash" with others, create your knitting library, show off your projects, and connect with other like-minded users in the hundreds of forums.

Knitty: www.knitty.com
The online magazine for knitters. Free patterns and fantastic articles.

Knitting Help: www.knittinghelp.com
A fantastic resource for beginner and advanced knitters alike. They have videos to help with learning new techniques.

acknowledgments

A special mention to my mum, Helen, who tried and tried, I am sure, to teach me to knit as a child. I can clearly remember requesting only pink yarn, please, and being delighted when my nan (a fantastic knitter) would give in when my mum wouldn't. Neither of them could teach me to knit, though.

Thank you also to my nan and papa (are you surprised, Papa?) for inspiring me with their handknits. I have a photo of the two of them on my parents' sofa, knitting away together in the evening. That image will be in my memory forever.

A big thank you to my husband, for the hours of pain and hardship he endured while I wrote this book. Thank you, honey.

Gemma, thank you for helping me keep my game on at the crazy photo shoot! I could not have done it without you.

Bec, for last minute babysitting (and pep talks) while I knit like a madwoman!

Sian, for all the coffee. And for listening to me rant and rave. And, well, for a million other things, too.

Thank you to my mother-in-law, Lesley, for helping me out when I was in a rush by sewing hearts onto hats or helping me knit.

And lastly, a HUGE thank you to all of the darling models! Without you little sweeties (and your wonderful parents) the hats would be no fun at all.

index